Airbnb Mortgage Loans for Multi-Unit Properties

How to Finance Duplexes, Triplexes, and Small Multifamily Airbnb Investments

By Joseph G. Correa

Licensed Mortgage Broker, Finibi Mortgage

Copyright & Legal Notice

Published by Live Stronger Faster

The information provided in this book is for educational and informational purposes only and should not be construed as financial, legal, or tax advice. Readers are encouraged to consult with licensed professionals before making any financial or real estate decisions. The author and publisher assume no responsibility for any losses or damages incurred as a result of the use or misuse of the information contained in this publication.

First Edition, 2026

Table of Contents

Foreword

The path to building long-term wealth through real estate has evolved, and few strategies have accelerated that evolution more than short-term rentals powered by platforms like Airbnb. What was once a niche opportunity has now become a highly scalable investment model capable of generating significantly higher income than traditional long-term rentals. Yet as the opportunity has grown, so has the complexity. Financing multi-unit Airbnb properties—duplexes, triplexes, and fourplexes—requires a deeper understanding of loan structures, income modeling, zoning laws, and strategic positioning than almost any other segment of real estate investing. This book is designed to give you that edge.

Multi-unit Airbnb investing sits at a powerful intersection. On one side, you have residential financing, which often provides more favorable terms, lower down payments, and more flexible underwriting than commercial loans. On the other side, you have income potential that begins to resemble small-scale hospitality or commercial operations. When properly executed, a 2–4 unit short-term rental property can outperform multiple single-family properties while maintaining financing advantages that most investors overlook. This is where sophisticated investors separate themselves from beginners—not by working harder, but by structuring smarter.

In this book, you will learn how to approach multi-unit Airbnb financing not just as a borrower, but as a strategist. The goal is not simply to get approved for a loan. The goal is to build a system that allows you to acquire, optimize, and scale properties that generate consistent cash flow while positioning you for long-term growth. Every decision—from how you classify the property to how you present income to a lender—affects your ability to move forward. This is especially true with duplexes, triplexes, and fourplexes, where small adjustments in strategy can dramatically impact loan eligibility and profitability.

One of the most important concepts you will master in this book is the idea of mixed rental models. Unlike single-family Airbnb properties, multi-unit properties offer flexibility. You can rent all units short-term, combine short-term and long-term rentals, or even occupy one unit while renting the others. Each approach has different implications for financing, cash flow, and risk management. Understanding how to structure your rental strategy in alignment with your loan program is one of the most powerful tools you will develop.

Another critical element is understanding how lenders view multi-unit Airbnb properties. Traditional underwriting often relies on long-term rental projections or borrower income, but modern loan programs—especially DSCR and Non-QM products—are increasingly adapting to short-term rental data. However, not all lenders interpret this data the same way. Some rely on market rent, others on short-term rental projections, and some blend both. Knowing how to position your deal with the right lender can be the difference between approval and denial.

Zoning and compliance also play a central role in multi-unit Airbnb investing. Unlike single-family homes, multi-unit properties often fall under stricter local regulations. Cities and counties may impose restrictions on short-term rentals, occupancy limits, licensing requirements, and even property use classifications. A property that looks perfect on paper can quickly become a liability if it does not meet local guidelines. This book will help you think proactively about compliance, so you can avoid costly mistakes and protect your investment.

As you move through this material, you will begin to see that multi-unit Airbnb investing is not just about buying property—it is about building a scalable system. Each property you acquire should strengthen your position, improve your cash flow, and expand your ability to acquire the next deal.

This requires discipline, planning, and a clear understanding of how financing, operations, and market dynamics work together.

You will also learn how to evaluate deals with a level of precision that most investors never reach. Instead of relying on surface-level metrics, you will analyze income potential, occupancy trends, average daily rates, and expense structures across multiple units. You will understand how to project income in a way that aligns with lender expectations while still reflecting real-world performance. This dual perspective—investor and lender—is what allows you to move confidently and consistently in this space.

Risk management is another key theme throughout this book. Multi-unit Airbnb properties can generate strong returns, but they also come with unique risks. Market fluctuations, regulatory changes, seasonal demand shifts, and operational challenges can all impact performance. The goal is not to avoid risk entirely, but to structure your deals in a way that minimizes downside while maximizing upside. This includes maintaining adequate reserves, selecting the right markets, and diversifying your rental strategies.

One of the most powerful advantages of multi-unit properties is efficiency. Instead of managing multiple scattered single-family homes, you can concentrate your operations in one location. This can reduce management costs, streamline maintenance, and improve guest experience. When combined with the right financing strategy, this efficiency can significantly accelerate your path to financial independence.

Throughout this book, you will also develop a deeper understanding of leverage. Real estate has always been one of the most effective ways to use borrowed capital to generate wealth, but multi-unit Airbnb investing takes this concept even further. By using financing strategically, you can control high-performing assets with relatively low capital, allowing your returns to compound over time. The key is to use leverage intelligently—balancing growth with sustainability.

Another important concept is scalability. Many investors get stuck after their first or second property because they do not understand how to structure their portfolio for growth. Multi-unit Airbnb properties provide a unique opportunity to scale faster, but only if you approach them with a long-term strategy. This includes understanding how lenders view multiple properties, how to manage your debt-to-income or DSCR ratios, and how to recycle capital effectively.

You will also explore how to position yourself as a strong borrower. This goes beyond credit scores and down payments.

It includes how you present your experience, how you document your rental strategy, and how you communicate the strength of your deal. Lenders are not just evaluating numbers—they are evaluating risk. The more effectively you can demonstrate control and understanding, the more opportunities you will unlock.

As you progress, you will begin to think differently about properties themselves. Instead of asking whether a property is "good" or "bad," you will ask whether it fits your strategy. Does it align with your financing options? Does it meet zoning requirements? Does it provide the flexibility you need to adapt over time? This shift in perspective is what transforms you from a reactive investor into a proactive one.

This book is not about theory. It is about execution. Every concept you learn is designed to be applied in real-world scenarios. Whether you are purchasing your first duplex or expanding into a portfolio of multi-unit properties, the principles in this book will guide you through each step of the process.

By the time you finish this introduction and move into the core chapters, you will begin to see multi-unit Airbnb properties not just as investments, but as strategic assets. Assets that can generate income, build equity, and create opportunities far beyond what traditional real estate investing offers.

The opportunity is real, but so is the complexity. Those who take the time to understand the details—financing structures, rental strategies, compliance requirements, and market dynamics—are the ones who succeed. This book is your roadmap to mastering that complexity and turning it into a competitive advantage.

Welcome to Book 9 of The Airbnb Mortgage Loan Mastery Series. This is where scale begins to accelerate, where strategy becomes essential, and where your ability to structure deals determines how far you can go.

Chapter 1

Understanding Multi-Unit Airbnb Financing Foundations

Multi-unit Airbnb investing represents one of the most powerful yet misunderstood opportunities in modern real estate. While many investors begin their journey with single-family homes, those who understand the mechanics of duplexes, triplexes, and fourplexes quickly realize that these property types offer a unique combination of scalability, efficiency, and financing advantages. The key to unlocking this potential lies in understanding how financing works specifically for 2–4 unit properties within the short-term rental ecosystem, and how to position these properties in a way that aligns both with lender expectations and real-world income performance.

At its core, a multi-unit property is still considered residential real estate when it consists of one to four units. This classification is critical because it allows investors to access residential loan programs rather than commercial financing, which often comes with higher rates, stricter terms, and larger down payment requirements. However, while the classification remains residential, the income potential behaves more like a hybrid between residential and commercial use, especially when the property is operated as a short-term rental. This dual nature is what creates opportunity, but also complexity.

When lenders evaluate a multi-unit Airbnb property, they are not simply looking at the number of units. They are analyzing how the property generates income, how stable that income is, and how it compares to the borrower's overall financial profile. In traditional financing, long-term rental income is often used, supported by leases or market rent appraisals. However, with short-term rentals, income becomes more dynamic. Nightly rates fluctuate, occupancy varies by season, and revenue can significantly exceed long-term rental projections if managed correctly. This introduces both upside potential and perceived risk from the lender's perspective.

One of the most important distinctions you must understand is how different loan types treat income. Conventional loans may still rely heavily on long-term rental comparables, even if your intent is to operate the property as an Airbnb. In contrast, DSCR (Debt Service Coverage Ratio) loans are specifically designed to evaluate the property's ability to generate enough income to cover its debt obligations. Some DSCR lenders are now incorporating short-term rental data, including average daily rates and occupancy projections, into their underwriting models. This shift has opened the door for investors to qualify based on the true income potential of the property rather than being limited by traditional rental assumptions. However, not all DSCR loans are created equal. Some lenders will cap income at long-term rental levels, while others will allow higher projections based on short-term rental analytics. Understanding which lenders fall into each category—and how to present your deal accordingly—is essential. A well-structured loan submission can significantly increase your chances of approval and improve your loan terms. This includes providing data from reputable short-term rental analysis tools, demonstrating market demand, and clearly outlining your operational strategy.

Another key factor in multi-unit financing is occupancy strategy. With a duplex, triplex, or fourplex, you have multiple ways to structure your rentals. You might choose to rent all units as short-term rentals, maximizing income potential but increasing operational complexity. Alternatively, you might adopt a hybrid model, where one or more units are rented long-term to provide stable baseline income, while the remaining units are operated as short-term rentals for higher returns. This hybrid approach can sometimes make lenders more comfortable, as it introduces an element of predictability into the income stream.

Owner-occupancy is another dimension that can dramatically affect financing options. If you choose to live in one of the units, you may qualify for primary residence loan programs, which often offer lower interest rates and reduced down payment requirements. This strategy, commonly known as house hacking, allows investors to enter the market with less capital while still benefiting from rental income. Over time, the property can be converted into a full investment property, further increasing its income potential.

Credit, reserves, and overall borrower strength also play a significant role in multi-unit Airbnb financing. Because short-term rental income can be perceived as less stable than traditional rental income, lenders often look for stronger borrower profiles to offset this risk. This may include higher credit scores, larger cash reserves, and a demonstrated ability to manage rental properties. Positioning yourself as a low-risk borrower can open doors to better loan programs and more favorable terms.

Appraisal methodology is another critical component. In a traditional appraisal, the value of a property is often based on comparable sales and long-term rental income. However, for Airbnb properties, especially multi-unit ones, this approach can undervalue the property's true income potential. Some lenders allow for appraisals that incorporate short-term rental data, sometimes referred to as "Airbnb appraisals" or "short-term rental income appraisals." These appraisals use data from platforms and analytics tools to estimate potential revenue, providing a more accurate picture of the property's value as an income-producing asset.

Zoning and legal compliance must also be considered from the very beginning. Multi-unit properties are more likely to fall under specific zoning regulations, and not all areas permit short-term rentals. Some cities require permits, impose occupancy limits, or restrict the number of units that can be used for short-term rentals. Failing to understand these regulations can result in fines, forced shutdowns, or reduced income potential. A successful investor approaches zoning as part of the deal analysis, not as an afterthought.

Another foundational concept is understanding expense structure. Multi-unit properties typically have higher operating costs than single-family homes, including utilities, maintenance, cleaning, and management. However, they also benefit from economies of scale. For example, managing four units in one location is often more efficient than managing four separate properties. This efficiency can improve net income and make the property more attractive from both an investment and lending perspective.

As you begin to integrate these concepts, you will see that multi-unit Airbnb financing is not just about meeting minimum requirements. It is about aligning multiple variables—property type, rental strategy, loan program, borrower profile, and market conditions—into a cohesive plan. Each decision you make influences the others, and the most successful investors are those who can see the bigger picture.

This chapter serves as your foundation. It is designed to shift your mindset from simply acquiring properties to strategically structuring them. The goal is not just to get approved for a loan, but to position yourself for long-term success. By understanding how lenders think, how income is evaluated, and how properties are classified, you gain the ability to navigate the system with confidence.

As you move forward, keep in mind that every deal is unique. There is no one-size-fits-all approach to multi-unit Airbnb financing. The strategies you learn in this book are tools, and your ability to apply them effectively will determine your results. With the right knowledge and preparation, multi-unit properties can become one of the most powerful vehicles for building wealth in today's real estate market.

Real-Life Math Example: Multi-Unit Airbnb Deal Analysis

Imagine an investor named Daniel who is evaluating a triplex property in a growing vacation market. The property consists of three separate units, each capable of being rented independently on a short-term basis. Daniel's goal is to determine whether the property will qualify for a DSCR loan and whether it will generate sufficient cash flow to justify the investment.

The purchase price of the property is $750,000. Daniel plans to put 25 percent down, which equals $187,500. This leaves a loan amount of $562,500. The lender offers an interest rate of 7.5 percent on a 30-year term. Based on these terms, Daniel calculates his monthly principal and interest payment to be approximately $3,935.

Next, Daniel estimates operating expenses. Property taxes are $9,000 per year, which equals $750 per month. Insurance costs $3,000 per year, or $250 per month. Utilities, including electricity, water, and internet, are estimated at $900 per month for all three units combined. Cleaning and maintenance average $1,200 per month, while property management, if used, would cost approximately 20 percent of gross revenue. For now, Daniel plans to self-manage, reducing this expense but increasing his time commitment.

Now Daniel turns to income projections. Using short-term rental data from the local market, he estimates that each unit can generate an average daily rate of $150 with an average occupancy of 70 percent. This means each unit is rented approximately 21 nights per month. Multiplying 21 nights by $150 results in $3,150 per unit per month. For three units, total gross monthly revenue is $9,450.

To calculate DSCR, Daniel first determines total monthly expenses. Adding the mortgage payment of $3,935, taxes of $750, insurance of $250, utilities of $900, and cleaning/maintenance of $1,200 results in total monthly expenses of $7,035. He then divides gross income of $9,450 by total expenses of $7,035, resulting in a DSCR of approximately 1.34.

Most DSCR lenders require a minimum ratio of 1.0 to 1.25, depending on the program. With a DSCR of 1.34, Daniel's deal appears to meet lender requirements. However, he also considers a more conservative scenario. If occupancy drops to 60 percent, each unit would generate $2,700 per month, for a total of $8,100. Dividing $8,100 by $7,035 results in a DSCR of 1.15, which may still qualify but offers less margin for error.

Daniel also evaluates cash flow. Subtracting total expenses of $7,035 from gross income of $9,450 leaves $2,415 in monthly cash flow before reserves and unexpected costs. Annually, this equates to approximately $28,980. Based on his initial investment of $187,500, this represents a cash-on-cash return of about 15.5 percent, which is strong compared to many traditional investments. To further strengthen his position, Daniel sets aside six months of reserves, totaling approximately $42,000. This provides a safety net in case of vacancies, market changes, or unexpected expenses. It also makes his loan application more attractive to the lender.

Through this analysis, Daniel gains a clear understanding of both the opportunity and the risks. He sees that the property has strong income potential and meets DSCR requirements, but he also recognizes the importance of maintaining occupancy and controlling expenses. By running both optimistic and conservative scenarios, he positions himself to make an informed decision.

This example illustrates how numbers drive every aspect of multi-unit Airbnb investing. From loan approval to long-term profitability, your ability to analyze and structure deals mathematically is what determines your success.

Chapter 2

Structuring the Perfect Multi-Unit Airbnb Deal

When it comes to multi-unit Airbnb investing, the difference between an average deal and an exceptional one is almost always found in the structure. Most investors focus heavily on finding properties and estimating income, but the true leverage lies in how the deal is put together from the beginning. Structuring the perfect multi-unit Airbnb deal requires aligning financing, rental strategy, property selection, and risk management into one cohesive plan. This chapter will teach you how to think like a strategist, not just a buyer.

The first principle of deal structuring is understanding that every variable affects your outcome. Purchase price, down payment, loan terms, interest rate, rental model, and operating costs are all interconnected. A small adjustment in one area can significantly impact your cash flow, DSCR, and long-term scalability. Successful investors do not look at these variables in isolation—they optimize them together.

One of the most important decisions you will make is how to classify the property at the time of purchase. Is it going to be positioned as a primary residence, a second home, or an investment property? Each classification comes with different financing options, down payment requirements, and interest rates. For example, purchasing a duplex as a primary residence may allow you to put as little as 5 percent down, while an investment property may require 20 to 25 percent. This decision alone can determine how quickly you can enter the market and how much capital you preserve for future deals.

House hacking is one of the most powerful strategies for structuring a multi-unit Airbnb deal. By living in one unit and renting out the others, you can reduce your personal housing costs while building equity and generating income. In some cases, the rental income from the other units can fully cover your mortgage, effectively allowing you to live for free. Over time, you can move out, convert the entire property into a short-term rental, and repeat the process with another property.

Another critical component of deal structuring is choosing the right loan product. Conventional loans, DSCR loans, and Non-QM loans each have their advantages and limitations. Conventional loans often offer lower interest rates but may restrict how rental income is calculated. DSCR loans provide more flexibility by focusing on the property's income rather than the borrower's personal income. Non-QM loans can accommodate unique situations, such as self-employed borrowers or investors with complex financial profiles. The key is to match the loan product to your strategy, not the other way around.

Interest rates and loan terms also play a major role in deal performance. A lower interest rate reduces your monthly payment, improving both cash flow and DSCR. However, some investors are willing to accept slightly higher rates in exchange for more flexible underwriting or faster approvals. Understanding this trade-off allows you to make decisions based on your overall strategy rather than focusing on a single variable.

Another essential aspect of structuring is the rental model itself. With multi-unit properties, you have the flexibility to design a strategy that maximizes both income and stability. Some investors choose to operate all units as short-term rentals, aiming for maximum revenue. Others prefer a hybrid model, where one or two units are rented long-term to provide consistent income, while the remaining units are used for short-term rentals to capture higher nightly rates. This hybrid approach can be particularly effective in markets with seasonal demand.

The concept of layering income streams is one of the most

powerful advantages of multi-unit properties. Instead of relying on a single source of income, you can create multiple revenue channels within the same property. This not only increases your total income but also reduces risk. If one unit experiences lower occupancy, the others can help offset the impact. From a lender's perspective, this diversification can make the property more attractive, especially if part of the income is stable and predictable.

Expense management is another area where structuring makes a significant difference. Multi-unit properties come with higher operating costs, but they also offer opportunities for efficiency. For example, utilities can often be consolidated, maintenance can be streamlined, and cleaning services can be scheduled more efficiently. By controlling expenses, you can improve your net operating income and strengthen your DSCR.

Reserves and liquidity are often overlooked but are critical to long-term success. Lenders may require a certain number of months of reserves, but experienced investors go beyond the minimum. Having sufficient reserves allows you to navigate unexpected challenges, such as temporary vacancies, repairs, or changes in market conditions. It also gives you the confidence to make strategic decisions without being forced into reactive ones.

Another key element of structuring is exit strategy. Before you even purchase the property, you should have a clear understanding of how you plan to exit or reposition the asset in the future. Will you refinance to pull out equity? Will you sell after increasing the property's value? Will you hold long-term for cash flow? Each of these strategies has implications for how you structure the deal initially.

Zoning and compliance must also be integrated into your deal structure. A property that generates strong projected income is only valuable if it can legally operate as a short-term rental. This means understanding local regulations, obtaining necessary permits, and ensuring that your property meets all requirements. Ignoring this step can turn a profitable deal into a costly mistake.

Another advanced concept in deal structuring is using partnerships or joint ventures. By combining resources with other investors, you can access larger deals, share risk, and scale more quickly. However, partnerships must be structured carefully, with clear agreements on roles, responsibilities, and profit distribution.

As you develop your ability to structure deals, you will begin to see opportunities that others miss. You will recognize properties that can be repositioned, income that can be optimized, and financing that can be tailored to your advantage. This is what separates experienced investors from beginners. Ultimately, structuring the perfect multi-unit Airbnb deal is about control. It is about controlling your financing, your income, your expenses, and your risk. When all of these elements are aligned, you create a deal that not only works on paper but performs in the real world.

This chapter is designed to give you the framework for thinking strategically. As you move forward, you will apply these principles to real scenarios, refining your ability to structure deals that support your long-term goals. The more intentional you are in this process, the more predictable your success will become.

Real-Life Math Example: Structuring a High-Performance Duplex Airbnb Deal

Consider an investor named Sophia who is analyzing a duplex in a strong short-term rental market. The purchase price of the property is $600,000. Sophia decides to use a primary residence loan and plans to occupy one unit while renting out the other. She puts 10 percent down, which equals $60,000, leaving a loan amount of $540,000.

Sophia secures a 30-year loan at an interest rate of 6.75 percent. Her monthly principal and interest payment is approximately $3,500. Property taxes are $7,200 per year, or $600 per month. Insurance costs $2,400 per year, or $200 per month. Utilities for the entire property are estimated at $600 per month, and maintenance averages $500 per month.

Sophia plans to rent out one unit as a short-term rental. Based on market data, she estimates an average daily rate of $180 with an occupancy rate of 65 percent. This results in approximately 19.5 booked nights per month, which she rounds to 20 nights. Multiplying 20 nights by $180 results in $3,600 in monthly gross income from the rental unit.

Her total monthly expenses are $3,500 (mortgage) + $600 (taxes) + $200 (insurance) + $600 (utilities) + $500 (maintenance), which equals $5,400. However, since she is living in one unit, she considers how much of these expenses are offset by rental income.

With $3,600 in rental income, Sophia effectively reduces her out-of-pocket housing cost to $1,800 per month. Compared to renting a similar property for $2,500 per month, she is already saving $700 per month while building equity.

Now Sophia considers converting the property into a full duplex Airbnb after moving out. If both units generate $3,600 per month, total gross income would be $7,200. Subtracting total expenses of $5,400 results in $1,800 in monthly cash flow. To evaluate DSCR, Sophia divides $7,200 by $5,400, resulting in a DSCR of 1.33. This meets typical lender requirements and positions her well for a future refinance.

Sophia also analyzes a conservative scenario. If occupancy drops to 55 percent, each unit generates approximately $3,000 per month, for a total of $6,000. Dividing $6,000 by $5,400 results in a DSCR of 1.11, which is still within acceptable limits for some lenders.

Sophia's initial investment of $60,000 generates $1,800 per month in cash flow once fully converted, which equals $21,600 per year. This represents a cash-on-cash return of 36 percent, demonstrating the power of combining strategic financing with short-term rental income.

By structuring the deal as a primary residence initially, Sophia reduced her down payment, improved her cash flow, and created a pathway to scale. She plans to repeat this strategy with another property, using the same approach to build a portfolio over time.

This example highlights how deal structure can dramatically impact both short-term performance and long-term growth. By aligning financing, rental strategy, and risk management, Sophia transforms a simple duplex into a high-performing investment.

Chapter 3

Analyzing Multi-Unit Airbnb Deals Like an Underwriter

The transition from beginner investor to advanced operator begins when you start analyzing deals the way a lender—or more specifically, an underwriter—does. Most investors evaluate properties based on surface-level metrics such as purchase price, estimated income, and rough cash flow. While these are important, they are only the starting point. True mastery comes from understanding how every number connects, how risk is interpreted, and how to present a deal that not only performs well in reality but also meets strict lending guidelines. In the world of multi-unit Airbnb investing, this level of analysis is not optional—it is essential.

An underwriter's primary objective is simple: determine whether the property can reliably support the debt being placed on it. This is where the concept of Debt Service Coverage Ratio becomes central. While investors often view DSCR as just a number to meet lender requirements, underwriters view it as a measure of risk. A higher DSCR indicates a greater margin of safety, while a lower DSCR suggests vulnerability to market fluctuations. As an investor, your goal is to structure and analyze your deal in a way that demonstrates strength, stability, and sustainability.

The first step in underwriting a multi-unit Airbnb deal is establishing realistic income projections. This is where many investors make critical mistakes. Overestimating occupancy, inflating nightly rates, or ignoring seasonality can lead to projections that look impressive on paper but fail in practice. Instead, you must rely on data-driven analysis. This includes reviewing comparable short-term rental properties, analyzing average daily rates, occupancy trends, and seasonal variations. The more grounded your projections are in reality, the stronger your position will be.

In multi-unit properties, income analysis becomes more complex but also more powerful. Each unit represents an individual income stream, and when combined, they create a layered revenue model. This allows for diversification within a single property. However, it also requires careful consideration of how each unit performs independently and collectively. An underwriter will often look at the overall income, but a sophisticated investor will break it down further, identifying strengths and weaknesses within each unit.

Expense analysis is equally critical. Many investors underestimate operating costs, particularly in short-term rental properties. Cleaning fees, maintenance, utilities, platform fees, and management costs can significantly impact net income. In multi-unit properties, these expenses are multiplied across units, but they can also be optimized through efficiency. For example, coordinating cleaning schedules, negotiating service contracts, and consolidating utilities can reduce overall costs. Understanding these dynamics allows you to present a more accurate and compelling financial picture.

Once income and expenses are established, the next step is calculating net operating income and comparing it to debt service. This is where DSCR is derived. However, beyond the calculation itself, the interpretation matters. A DSCR of 1.25 may meet minimum requirements, but a DSCR of 1.40 or higher provides a stronger cushion against uncertainty. As an investor, you should always aim to exceed minimum thresholds, creating a margin of safety that protects your investment.

Another important factor in underwriting is stress testing your deal. This involves analyzing how the property performs under less favorable conditions. What happens if occupancy drops by 10 percent? What if nightly rates decline due to increased competition? What if expenses increase unexpectedly? By modeling these scenarios, you gain a deeper understanding of your risk exposure and can make more informed decisions. Underwriters often perform similar analyses, so anticipating these scenarios strengthens your position. Market analysis also plays a significant role. Not all markets are equally suited for multi-unit Airbnb properties. Factors such as tourism demand, local regulations, seasonality, and competition all influence performance. A strong market can compensate for minor inefficiencies in a deal, while a weak market can undermine even the most well-structured investment. As an investor, you must evaluate both the property and the market in which it operates.

Loan structure is another variable that directly impacts underwriting. Interest rate, loan term, and down payment all affect your monthly payment and, consequently, your DSCR. A lower interest rate or higher down payment can improve your ratio, making the deal more attractive to lenders. However, these decisions must be balanced against your overall investment strategy. For example, a higher down payment may improve DSCR but reduce your ability to acquire additional properties.

Reserves and liquidity are often considered the final layer of underwriting. Lenders want to see that you have the financial capacity to handle unexpected challenges. This includes having sufficient cash reserves to cover several months of expenses. From an investor's perspective, reserves provide peace of mind and flexibility. They allow you to navigate fluctuations without being forced into unfavorable decisions. Another advanced concept in underwriting multi-unit Airbnb deals is understanding how different lenders interpret the same data. Some lenders may be more conservative, relying heavily on long-term rental comparables, while others may embrace short-term rental projections. Knowing how to align your deal with the right lender can significantly improve your chances of approval. This is where experience and preparation become invaluable.

As you develop your underwriting skills, you will begin to see deals differently. Instead of asking whether a property "looks good," you will ask whether it performs under scrutiny. You will identify potential weaknesses before they become problems and structure your deals to address them proactively. This shift in mindset is what separates successful investors from those who struggle.

Ultimately, analyzing multi-unit Airbnb deals like an underwriter is about clarity and precision. It is about understanding every number, every assumption, and every risk. When you approach deals with this level of discipline, you gain control over your outcomes. You are no longer guessing—you are making informed, strategic decisions.

This chapter is your guide to developing that level of expertise. As you move forward, you will apply these principles to real-world scenarios, refining your ability to evaluate and structure deals with confidence. The more you practice this approach, the more natural it will become, and the more successful you will be in building a high-performing Airbnb portfolio.

Real-Life Math Example: Underwriting a Fourplex Airbnb Investment

Consider an investor named Marcus who is evaluating a fourplex property in a high-demand vacation market. The purchase price is $920,000. Marcus plans to use a DSCR loan with a 25 percent down payment, which equals $230,000. This results in a loan amount of $690,000.

Marcus secures a 30-year loan at an interest rate of 7.25 percent. His monthly principal and interest payment is approximately $4,710. Property taxes are $11,040 per year, or $920 per month. Insurance costs $3,600 per year, or $300 per month. Utilities for all four units are estimated at $1,200 per month. Cleaning and maintenance average $1,800 per month.

Marcus begins by analyzing income. Based on market data, each unit has an average daily rate of $165 with an occupancy rate of 68 percent. This results in approximately 20.4 booked nights per month per unit, which Marcus rounds to 20 nights for conservative estimates. Multiplying 20 nights by $165 results in $3,300 per unit per month. For four units, total gross monthly income is $13,200.

Next, Marcus calculates total monthly expenses. Adding the mortgage payment of $4,710, taxes of $920, insurance of $300, utilities of $1,200, and cleaning/maintenance of $1,800 results in total expenses of $8,930 per month.

To calculate DSCR, Marcus divides gross income of $13,200 by total expenses of $8,930, resulting in a DSCR of approximately 1.48. This exceeds typical lender requirements and provides a strong margin of safety.

Marcus then stress tests the deal. If occupancy drops to 60 percent, each unit generates approximately $2,970 per month, resulting in total income of $11,880. Dividing $11,880 by $8,930 results in a DSCR of 1.33, which still meets most lender requirements.

He also considers a scenario where both occupancy drops to 60 percent and average daily rate declines to $150. In this case, each unit generates $2,700 per month, for a total of $10,800. Dividing $10,800 by $8,930 results in a DSCR of 1.21. While this is lower, it may still qualify depending on the lender.

Marcus evaluates cash flow as well. At the original projections, subtracting expenses of $8,930 from income of $13,200 results in $4,270 in monthly cash flow. Annually, this equals $51,240. Based on his investment of $230,000, this represents a cash-on-cash return of approximately 22.3 percent.

Marcus also sets aside reserves equal to six months of expenses, totaling approximately $53,580. This strengthens his loan application and provides a financial buffer.

Through this detailed underwriting process, Marcus gains confidence in the deal. He understands not only its potential but also its risks. By analyzing multiple scenarios and aligning his strategy with lender expectations, he positions himself for both approval and long-term success.

This example demonstrates how thinking like an underwriter transforms your approach to investing. Instead of relying on assumptions, you rely on data, analysis, and strategic planning—creating a foundation for consistent and scalable growth.

Chapter 4

Zoning, Compliance, and Legal Strategy for Multi-Unit Airbnb Properties

One of the most overlooked yet critical components of multi-unit Airbnb investing is zoning and compliance. While financing, income projections, and deal structuring often receive the most attention, the reality is that none of those elements matter if the property cannot legally operate as a short-term rental. This is especially true for duplexes, triplexes, and fourplexes, where regulations tend to be stricter and more complex than for single-family homes. Understanding how to navigate zoning laws, local ordinances, and compliance requirements is not just a defensive strategy—it is a competitive advantage.

Zoning determines how a property can be used. At a basic level, properties are classified into categories such as residential, commercial, or mixed-use. Multi-unit properties typically fall under residential zoning, but this does not automatically mean they can be used for short-term rentals. Many cities and counties have introduced specific regulations governing short-term rentals, often requiring permits, limiting occupancy, or restricting the number of units that can be rented on a short-term basis. In some cases, entire zones may prohibit short-term rentals altogether.

The complexity increases with multi-unit properties because they can be interpreted differently depending on local laws. A duplex may be treated similarly to a single-family home in one jurisdiction, while in another it may be subject to additional restrictions. Triplexes and fourplexes often fall into a gray area, where they are still considered residential for financing purposes but may be regulated more like small commercial properties for operational use. This dual classification requires investors to be extremely diligent in their research.

One of the first steps in evaluating a property is verifying whether short-term rentals are permitted in that specific location. This involves reviewing local zoning codes, municipal ordinances, and, in some cases, homeowners association rules. Many cities provide online resources where you can search property addresses and view zoning classifications. However, these tools are not always sufficient. It is often necessary to contact local planning departments directly to confirm the latest regulations and any upcoming changes.

Permitting is another key aspect of compliance. Even in areas where short-term rentals are allowed, you may be required to obtain a permit or license to operate legally. This process can include submitting an application, paying fees, undergoing inspections, and meeting specific requirements such as safety standards and occupancy limits. For multi-unit properties, permits may be required for each unit individually, or there may be a cap on the number of units that can be operated as short-term rentals within a single property.

Occupancy regulations are particularly important in multi-unit Airbnb investing. Local laws often limit the number of guests per unit based on factors such as square footage, number of bedrooms, and safety considerations. Exceeding these limits can result in fines or revocation of your permit. As an investor, you must design your rental strategy within these constraints, ensuring that your income projections are realistic and compliant.

Another critical consideration is tax compliance. Short-term rental income is often subject to local lodging taxes, which may include transient occupancy taxes, sales taxes, or tourism taxes. These taxes can vary significantly by location and must be factored into your financial analysis. Some platforms automatically collect and remit certain taxes, but this is not always the case. It is your responsibility to understand your obligations and ensure that all taxes are properly reported and paid. Insurance is also a key component of legal strategy. Standard homeowner's insurance policies may not cover short-term rental activity, especially in multi-unit properties.

You may need specialized insurance that includes liability coverage for guests, property damage, and loss of income. This is particularly important in multi-unit properties, where the risk exposure is higher due to multiple tenants and increased guest turnover.

Noise, parking, and community impact regulations are becoming increasingly common as short-term rentals grow in popularity. Local governments often implement rules to address concerns from neighbors, such as noise complaints, parking congestion, and property maintenance. These regulations can include quiet hours, designated parking requirements, and restrictions on events or gatherings. As an investor, maintaining good relationships with neighbors and adhering to these rules can help protect your business and prevent conflicts.

One of the most strategic approaches to zoning and compliance is selecting markets that are favorable to short-term rentals. Some cities actively support short-term rental activity, recognizing its economic benefits, while others impose strict limitations. By focusing on markets with clear and supportive regulations, you reduce risk and increase your chances of long-term success. This requires not only understanding current laws but also anticipating future trends and regulatory changes. Another advanced strategy is structuring your property and operations in a way that aligns with local regulations. For example, if a city limits the number of short-term rental permits, you may choose to operate some units as long-term rentals while keeping others as short-term. This hybrid approach allows you to remain compliant while still maximizing income. Similarly, you may structure ownership through an entity that provides liability protection and operational flexibility.

Legal agreements and documentation also play a role in compliance. Guest agreements, house rules, and disclosures can help protect you from liability and ensure that guests understand their responsibilities. In multi-unit properties, clear communication is essential to maintaining order and preventing issues that could lead to regulatory scrutiny.

As you gain experience, you will begin to see zoning and compliance not as obstacles but as filters. They help you identify which deals are viable and which are not. A property with strong income potential but poor compliance prospects is not a good investment. Conversely, a property in a well-regulated, supportive market may offer long-term stability and growth.

Ultimately, mastering zoning and compliance is about control. It is about ensuring that your business operates within the law while maximizing its potential. Investors who ignore this aspect often face setbacks that could have been avoided. Those who embrace it gain a significant advantage, positioning themselves for sustainable success.

This chapter provides you with the framework to navigate the legal landscape of multi-unit Airbnb investing. As you apply these principles, you will develop the ability to evaluate properties not just based on numbers, but on their legal viability. This is a critical step in building a portfolio that is both profitable and resilient.

Real-Life Math Example: Compliance Impact on Multi-Unit Airbnb Income

Consider an investor named Elena who is analyzing a fourplex property in a city with moderate short-term rental regulations. The purchase price is $800,000, and she plans to use a DSCR loan with a 25 percent down payment of $200,000, resulting in a loan amount of $600,000. Her monthly mortgage payment is approximately $4,200. Property taxes are $10,000 per year, or $833 per month, and insurance costs $3,200 per year, or $267 per month. Utilities and maintenance combined are estimated at $2,000 per month.

Initially, Elena plans to operate all four units as short-term rentals. Based on market data, each unit is expected to generate $3,000 per month, resulting in total gross income of $12,000. Total monthly expenses are $4,200 (mortgage) + $833 (taxes) + $267 (insurance) + $2,000 (utilities/maintenance), which equals $7,300. This results in a projected cash flow of $4,700 per month and a DSCR of approximately 1.64.

However, Elena discovers that local regulations limit short-term rentals to two units per property unless a special permit is obtained, which is currently capped and unavailable. This forces her to adjust her strategy. She decides to operate two units as short-term rentals and rent the remaining two units long-term at $1,800 per month each.

Under this new structure, the two short-term units generate $3,000 each, totaling $6,000. The two long-term units generate $1,800 each, totaling $3,600. Combined gross monthly income is now $9,600.

Recalculating her numbers, Elena subtracts total expenses of $7,300 from income of $9,600, resulting in $2,300 in monthly cash flow. Her DSCR is now $9,600 divided by $7,300, which equals approximately 1.32. While this is lower than her original projection, it still meets lender requirements and provides positive cash flow.

Elena also considers a conservative scenario where short-term rental income drops by 10 percent and one long-term tenant vacates for a month. In this case, short-term income decreases to $5,400, and long-term income drops to $1,800 for that month, resulting in total income of $7,200. Dividing $7,200 by $7,300 results in a DSCR of 0.99, which is below lender requirements but only temporary.

To mitigate this risk, Elena sets aside six months of reserves totaling $43,800. She also explores the possibility of obtaining a permit in the future or increasing long-term rents as the market grows.

This example demonstrates how zoning and compliance directly impact financial performance. By adjusting her strategy to align with local regulations, Elena transforms a potentially non-compliant deal into a sustainable investment. While her income is reduced, her risk is also managed, and her property remains legally operational.

Understanding how to adapt your numbers based on real-world constraints is a critical skill. It ensures that your investment is not only profitable on paper but viable in practice, allowing you to build a portfolio that stands the test of time.

Chapter 5

Optimizing Income and Cash Flow in Multi-Unit Airbnb Properties

Once a multi-unit Airbnb property is acquired and properly financed, the next phase—and arguably the most important for long-term success—is optimization. This is where average deals become exceptional assets. Many investors make the mistake of assuming that income is fixed once a property is purchased, but in reality, income is highly dynamic. With the right strategies, systems, and adjustments, a multi-unit property can significantly outperform its initial projections. This chapter is focused on showing you how to maximize income, stabilize cash flow, and create a property that consistently produces strong financial results.

The foundation of income optimization begins with understanding revenue drivers. In short-term rental properties, the two most important variables are average daily rate (ADR) and occupancy. These two factors work together to determine total revenue, but they are not independent. Increasing your nightly rate may reduce occupancy, while lowering your rate may increase bookings but reduce overall revenue. The goal is to find the optimal balance that maximizes total income, not just one metric. In multi-unit properties, this becomes even more powerful because you are not relying on a single unit. Each unit can be optimized individually based on its size, layout, and target audience. For example, one unit may be positioned as a premium listing with higher rates and lower occupancy, while another may focus on affordability and higher occupancy. This segmentation allows you to capture different segments of the market and diversify your income streams within the same property.

Dynamic pricing is one of the most effective tools for maximizing revenue. Instead of setting a fixed nightly rate, dynamic pricing adjusts your rates based on demand, seasonality, local events, and market trends. This ensures that you are charging the highest possible rate during peak periods while remaining competitive during slower times. Investors who implement dynamic pricing often see significant increases in revenue without any changes to the property itself.

Another critical component of income optimization is listing quality. High-quality photos, compelling descriptions, and strong reviews all contribute to higher booking rates and the ability to charge premium prices. In multi-unit properties, consistency across units is important, but so is differentiation. Each unit should have its own identity while maintaining a cohesive brand. This not only improves guest experience but also increases visibility on booking platforms. Guest experience plays a direct role in income. Properties that consistently receive high ratings are more likely to be booked, can command higher rates, and experience fewer vacancies. This includes everything from cleanliness and communication to amenities and overall presentation. Small upgrades, such as better furnishings, faster internet, or thoughtful touches like welcome packages, can have a disproportionate impact on guest satisfaction and revenue.

Another advanced strategy is length-of-stay optimization. While short stays can maximize nightly rates, longer stays can reduce turnover costs and provide more stable income. By adjusting your pricing strategy, you can encourage longer bookings during slower periods while maintaining flexibility during high-demand times. This balance helps stabilize cash flow and reduce operational strain.

Expense optimization is equally important. Increasing revenue is only one side of the equation—controlling costs is the other. In multi-unit properties, there are opportunities to reduce expenses through efficiency. For example, bulk purchasing supplies, scheduling cleanings back-to-back, and consolidating services can lower overall costs. Technology can also play a role, with automation tools reducing the time and effort required to manage bookings, communication, and operations. Utilities are often one of the largest variable expenses in multi-unit Airbnb properties. Implementing energy-efficient systems, smart thermostats, and usage monitoring can significantly reduce costs. Additionally, setting clear house rules and educating guests can help prevent excessive usage. Over time, these small adjustments can lead to meaningful savings.

Another key concept is revenue layering. Beyond nightly bookings, there are additional ways to generate income from your property. This can include charging for early check-ins or late check-outs, offering premium amenities, or partnering with local services such as tours or transportation. While these additional revenue streams may seem small individually, they can add up significantly over time.

Seasonality is another factor that must be managed carefully. Most markets experience fluctuations in demand throughout the year. Understanding these patterns allows you to adjust your strategy accordingly. During peak seasons, you can maximize rates and occupancy. During slower periods, you can focus on maintaining bookings through competitive pricing, longer stays, or targeted marketing.

Cash flow management is the ultimate goal of all these strategies. Positive cash flow provides stability, allows for reinvestment, and reduces financial stress. However, it is important to think beyond monthly cash flow and consider long-term performance. This includes building reserves, planning for capital expenditures, and continuously reinvesting in the property to maintain its competitiveness.

Another advanced concept is portfolio-level optimization. As you acquire more properties, you can begin to manage them as a system rather than individually. This includes standardizing operations, sharing resources, and leveraging data across properties to improve performance. Multi-unit properties are particularly well-suited for this approach, as they already contain multiple income streams within a single asset.

Scaling also requires discipline. It is not enough to simply increase income—you must ensure that your systems can support growth. This includes having reliable processes for cleaning, maintenance, guest communication, and financial tracking. Without these systems, increased income can be offset by increased complexity and risk.

Ultimately, optimizing income and cash flow is about continuous improvement. Markets change, competition evolves, and guest expectations shift. The most successful investors arc those who adapt, test new strategies, and refine their approach over time. By treating your property as a business rather than a static investment, you position yourself for sustained success. This chapter provides the framework for maximizing the performance of your multi-unit Airbnb property. By focusing on both revenue and expenses, and by leveraging the unique advantages of multi-unit properties, you can create a high-performing asset that generates consistent and growing income.

Real-Life Math Example: Optimizing a Triplex Airbnb for Maximum Cash Flow

Consider an investor named Javier who owns a triplex property purchased for $720,000. He put 25 percent down, investing $180,000, and financed the remaining $540,000 at a 7 percent interest rate. His monthly mortgage payment is approximately $3,600. Property taxes are $8,640 per year, or $720 per month, and insurance costs $2,880 per year, or $240 per month. Utilities and maintenance total $1,500 per month.

Initially, Javier operates all three units with a fixed pricing strategy. Each unit generates an average of $2,800 per month, resulting in total gross income of $8,400. His total monthly expenses are $3,600 (mortgage) + $720 (taxes) + $240 (insurance) + $1,500 (utilities/maintenance), which equals $6,060. This results in a monthly cash flow of $2,340.

Javier then decides to implement optimization strategies. He introduces dynamic pricing, improves listing quality, and enhances guest experience. As a result, his average daily rate increases, and occupancy improves. Each unit now generates $3,300 per month, increasing total gross income to $9,900.

With expenses remaining relatively stable at $6,060, Javier's monthly cash flow increases to $3,840. This represents an increase of $1,500 per month, or $18,000 per year, without any major capital investment.

Javier also identifies opportunities to reduce expenses. By optimizing cleaning schedules and negotiating service contracts, he reduces maintenance and cleaning costs by $300 per month. His new total expenses are $5,760, further increasing cash flow to $4,140 per month.

To evaluate DSCR, Javier divides income of $9,900 by expenses of $5,760, resulting in a DSCR of approximately 1.72. This strong ratio positions him well for future refinancing or expansion.

Javier then analyzes a conservative scenario. If income drops by 15 percent due to market conditions, each unit generates approximately $2,805 per month, resulting in total income of $8,415. Dividing $8,415 by $5,760 results in a DSCR of 1.46, which still provides a comfortable margin.

Annually, Javier's optimized property generates approximately $49,680 in cash flow. Based on his initial investment of $180,000, this represents a cash-on-cash return of 27.6 percent.

This example demonstrates the power of optimization. By focusing on both increasing revenue and reducing expenses, Javier transforms a solid investment into a high-performing asset. The key takeaway is that income is not fixed—it can be improved through strategy, execution, and continuous refinement.

When applied consistently, these principles can significantly accelerate your progress, allowing you to build a portfolio of properties that generate strong, reliable cash flow over time.

Chapter 6

Scaling a Multi-Unit Airbnb Portfolio with Smart Financing

Once you understand how to acquire and optimize a single multi-unit Airbnb property, the next level of growth comes from scaling. Scaling is where real wealth is built, but it is also where many investors get stuck. The challenge is not just finding more deals—it is structuring your financing, cash flow, and strategy in a way that allows you to repeat the process consistently without running out of capital or hitting lending limitations. This chapter is focused on how to scale intelligently using multi-unit properties as the foundation of your portfolio.

The first concept to understand is that scaling is not linear—it is exponential when done correctly. A single duplex may generate solid income, but a portfolio of duplexes, triplexes, and fourplexes can create a compounding effect where each property contributes to the acquisition of the next. The key is to create a system where your properties fund your growth rather than relying solely on your personal income or savings.

Financing plays the central role in this process. Most investors begin with conventional loans or primary residence strategies, but as they scale, they transition into DSCR loans, portfolio loans, and other investor-focused products. These loan types allow you to qualify based on property income rather than personal income, which removes one of the biggest barriers to scaling. However, each lender has limits, guidelines, and preferences, so understanding how to navigate these is critical.

One of the most powerful strategies for scaling is the BRRRR method—Buy, Rehab, Rent, Refinance, Repeat. While traditionally used in long-term rentals, it can be adapted for Airbnb properties. The idea is to acquire a property, improve it to increase its income potential, stabilize it as a short-term rental, and then refinance based on its higher value and income. This allows you to pull out equity and redeploy it into the next deal.

Multi-unit properties enhance this strategy because they generate more income per property, which can support higher valuations and stronger refinance opportunities. For example, increasing the performance of a fourplex can significantly impact its appraised value, especially if short-term rental income is considered. This creates opportunities to access capital without selling the asset.

Another key concept is capital recycling. Instead of letting your equity sit idle, you use refinancing, cash-out strategies, or lines of credit to reinvest into additional properties. This allows you to grow your portfolio faster without constantly injecting new personal funds. However, this must be done carefully to avoid over-leveraging. Maintaining a balance between growth and stability is essential.

Loan stacking is another advanced strategy. This involves using multiple lenders and loan products to acquire properties simultaneously or in quick succession. For example, you might use a conventional loan for one property, a DSCR loan for another, and a portfolio loan for a third. By diversifying your financing sources, you avoid hitting limits with any single lender and increase your ability to scale.

Debt management becomes increasingly important as your portfolio grows. Each loan adds to your overall obligations, and while DSCR loans focus on property income, your overall financial profile still matters. Keeping your ratios healthy, maintaining reserves, and ensuring that each property performs independently are key to sustaining growth.

Another important factor is building relationships with lenders. As you complete more deals, lenders begin to see you as a repeat investor rather than a one-time borrower. This can lead to better terms, faster approvals, and more flexibility. In some cases, lenders may even offer portfolio-level financing, allowing you to bundle multiple properties into a single loan. Portfolio diversification is also critical. While multi-unit Airbnb properties are powerful, relying on a single market or strategy can increase risk. Expanding into different markets, property types, or rental models can provide stability and reduce exposure to localized issues such as regulatory changes or market downturns.

Operational scalability must also be considered. As you acquire more properties, managing them individually becomes increasingly complex. Systems, automation, and possibly team members become necessary. This includes property management, cleaning services, maintenance coordination, and financial tracking. Without these systems, scaling can lead to inefficiencies and reduced performance.

Another advanced concept is portfolio optimization. Instead of viewing each property independently, you begin to manage your portfolio as a whole. This includes analyzing overall cash flow, balancing high-performing and stable properties, and making strategic decisions about refinancing, selling, or reinvesting. This holistic approach allows you to maximize returns while managing risk.

Exit strategies also evolve as you scale. While your initial focus may be on acquisition, long-term success requires planning for eventual exits. This could include selling properties at peak value, refinancing into more favorable terms, or transitioning into different types of investments. Having a clear exit strategy ensures that your portfolio remains aligned with your goals.

Tax strategy becomes increasingly important as well. Short-term rental income can have different tax implications than long-term rentals, and multi-unit properties add another layer of complexity. Working with a knowledgeable tax professional can help you optimize deductions, manage depreciation, and structure your portfolio in a tax-efficient manner.

As you continue to grow, mindset becomes a key factor. Scaling requires patience, discipline, and a willingness to adapt. Not every deal will be perfect, and not every strategy will work in every market. The most successful investors are those who learn from each experience and continuously refine their approach.

Ultimately, scaling a multi-unit Airbnb portfolio is about creating a system that works. It is about aligning financing, operations, and strategy in a way that allows you to grow consistently without compromising stability. When done correctly, this approach can lead to significant wealth creation and financial independence.

This chapter provides the blueprint for scaling. By applying these principles, you can move beyond individual deals and begin building a portfolio that generates consistent income and long-term value. The journey from one property to many is not just about growth—it is about transformation.

Real-Life Math Example: Scaling from One Fourplex to a Portfolio

Consider an investor named Andre who starts with a single fourplex purchased for $900,000. He puts 25 percent down, investing $225,000, and finances the remaining $675,000 at a 7.25 percent interest rate. His monthly mortgage payment is approximately $4,800. Property taxes are $10,800 per year ($900 per month), insurance is $3,600 per year ($300 per month), and operating expenses total $2,000 per month.

Each of the four units generates $3,200 per month in short-term rental income, resulting in total gross income of $12,800. Total monthly expenses are $4,800 (mortgage) + $900 (taxes) + $300 (insurance) + $2,000 (operations), which equals $8,000. This results in a monthly cash flow of $4,800.

After one year of optimization, Andre increases income to $14,000 per month through dynamic pricing and improved operations. His expenses remain stable at $8,000, increasing cash flow to $6,000 per month, or $72,000 per year.

The property is then reappraised based on its income performance and increased market value, now valued at $1,050,000. Andre refinances at 75 percent loan-to-value, resulting in a new loan of $787,500. After paying off the original loan of $675,000, he pulls out $112,500 in cash.

Andre combines this with savings and uses $150,000 to acquire a second property—a triplex priced at $600,000. He puts 25 percent down ($150,000) and finances the rest. The new property generates $9,000 per month in income with $6,000 in expenses, producing $3,000 in monthly cash flow.

Now Andre owns two properties generating a combined cash flow of $9,000 per month. Over time, he repeats this process, refinancing and reinvesting to acquire additional properties.

After acquiring a third property with similar performance, his portfolio generates approximately $13,000 per month in cash flow. Annually, this equals $156,000, created through strategic scaling rather than relying on a single asset.

Andre maintains reserves equal to six months of expenses for each property, ensuring stability. He also diversifies across different markets to reduce risk.

This example illustrates how scaling works in practice. By leveraging one property into multiple acquisitions, Andre transforms his initial investment into a growing portfolio. The key is not just acquiring properties, but using financing and income strategically to fuel continuous growth. When applied consistently, this approach allows investors to move from owning a single property to building a portfolio that generates substantial income and long-term wealth.

Chapter 7

Risk Management and Long-Term Stability in Multi-Unit Airbnb Investing

As your portfolio of multi-unit Airbnb properties grows, so does your exposure to risk. While earlier chapters focused on acquisition, structuring, and scaling, this chapter is about protecting what you build. The difference between investors who achieve long-term success and those who struggle often comes down to how well they manage risk. Multi-unit Airbnb properties can generate strong income, but they also introduce variables that must be controlled, anticipated, and mitigated.

Risk in short-term rental investing is not a single factor—it is a combination of market risk, operational risk, financial risk, and regulatory risk. Each of these areas must be addressed proactively. Ignoring even one can disrupt your entire portfolio. The goal is not to eliminate risk completely, which is impossible, but to create systems that reduce its impact and allow your portfolio to remain stable under changing conditions.

Market risk is one of the most significant factors. Short-term rental demand can fluctuate based on tourism trends, economic conditions, seasonality, and competition. A market that performs well today may face increased competition tomorrow, reducing occupancy and average daily rates. Multi-unit properties amplify this effect because a decline in demand affects multiple units simultaneously. To manage this risk, you must choose markets carefully, focusing on areas with diverse demand drivers such as tourism, business travel, events, and population growth.

Diversification is a key strategy for reducing market risk. Instead of concentrating all your properties in one location, you can spread your investments across different cities or regions. This ensures that a downturn in one market does not impact your entire portfolio. Additionally, within a single property, you can diversify by using mixed rental strategies, combining short-term and long-term rentals to create more stable income streams.

Operational risk is another critical area. Managing a multi-unit Airbnb property involves multiple moving parts, including guest communication, cleaning, maintenance, and scheduling. Any breakdown in these processes can lead to negative reviews, reduced bookings, and lost income. As your portfolio grows, manual management becomes increasingly difficult. Implementing systems and automation is essential to maintaining consistency and efficiency. Technology plays a major role in reducing operational risk. Automated messaging systems, booking management platforms, and dynamic pricing tools can streamline operations and reduce human error. Standardized processes for cleaning, maintenance, and guest interactions ensure that each unit performs consistently, regardless of scale. Building a reliable team, whether in-house or outsourced, further strengthens your operational stability.

Financial risk is closely tied to leverage. While financing allows you to scale, it also introduces obligations that must be met regardless of market conditions. High leverage can amplify returns, but it can also increase vulnerability during downturns. Maintaining a balanced approach to debt is essential. This includes ensuring that each property generates sufficient cash flow, maintaining healthy DSCR levels, and avoiding overextension.

Reserves are one of the most effective tools for managing financial risk. Having sufficient cash reserves allows you to cover expenses during periods of low occupancy or unexpected costs. Most lenders require a minimum number of months of reserves, but experienced investors often go beyond these requirements. A strong reserve position provides flexibility and peace of mind, allowing you to make strategic decisions rather than reacting under pressure.

Interest rate risk is another factor to consider, especially when using adjustable-rate loans or refinancing strategies. Changes in interest rates can impact your monthly payments and overall profitability. Locking in favorable rates when possible and stress testing your deals against higher rates can help mitigate this risk.

Regulatory risk is particularly relevant in the short-term rental industry. Laws and regulations can change, sometimes quickly, affecting your ability to operate. Multi-unit properties are often more heavily scrutinized, making compliance even more important. Staying informed about local regulations, maintaining proper permits, and adapting your strategy as needed are essential to long-term stability.

Insurance is a critical component of risk management. Standard policies may not cover all aspects of short-term rental activity, especially in multi-unit properties. Comprehensive coverage that includes liability, property damage, and loss of income is necessary to protect your investment. In addition, requiring security deposits and implementing clear house rules can reduce the likelihood of costly incidents.

Another important aspect of risk management is reputation. In the Airbnb ecosystem, reviews directly impact your income.

Negative reviews can reduce bookings and force you to lower your rates. Maintaining high standards of cleanliness, communication, and guest experience is essential to protecting your reputation. This is especially important in multi-unit properties, where a single issue can affect multiple units and guests.

Scenario planning is a powerful tool for managing risk. By analyzing different scenarios, such as occupancy declines, expense increases, or regulatory changes, you can prepare for potential challenges. This proactive approach allows you to identify weaknesses in your strategy and address them before they become problems.

Portfolio-level risk management is the next step as you scale. Instead of evaluating risk at the property level, you assess your entire portfolio. This includes analyzing overall cash flow, debt levels, market exposure, and operational capacity. Balancing high-performing properties with stable ones, maintaining reserves across the portfolio, and diversifying strategies all contribute to long-term stability.

Exit strategies also play a role in risk management. Having a clear plan for each property, whether it involves refinancing, selling, or converting to a different rental model, provides flexibility. This allows you to adapt to changing conditions and capitalize on opportunities.

Ultimately, risk management is about control and preparation. It is about building a portfolio that can withstand fluctuations and continue to perform over time. Investors who focus only on growth often overlook this aspect, while those who prioritize stability create lasting success.

This chapter provides the framework for protecting your investments. By understanding and managing risk across multiple dimensions, you can build a portfolio that not only grows but endures. The goal is not just to achieve success, but to sustain it.

Real-Life Math Example: Stress Testing a Multi-Unit Airbnb Portfolio

Consider an investor named Lucas who owns two multi-unit Airbnb properties: a duplex and a fourplex. The duplex generates $7,000 per month in income with $4,500 in expenses, resulting in $2,500 in cash flow. The fourplex generates $14,000 per month with $9,000 in expenses, resulting in $5,000 in cash flow. Combined, Lucas's portfolio generates $21,000 in income and $13,500 in expenses, producing $7,500 in monthly cash flow.

Lucas begins by analyzing his baseline DSCR. Dividing total income of $21,000 by total expenses of $13,500 results in a DSCR of approximately 1.56. This indicates a strong position under normal conditions. Next, Lucas stress tests his portfolio. He considers a scenario where occupancy drops by 20 percent due to a market slowdown. Income decreases to $16,800 per month. Expenses remain at $13,500, reducing cash flow to $3,300. The new DSCR is $16,800 divided by $13,500, which equals approximately 1.24. While still above minimum thresholds, the margin of safety is reduced.

Lucas then evaluates a more severe scenario. In addition to the 20 percent drop in income, expenses increase by $1,000 per month due to maintenance issues. Total expenses rise to $14,500, while income remains at $16,800. Cash flow drops to $2,300, and DSCR falls to approximately 1.16.

In a worst-case scenario, Lucas assumes a 30 percent drop in income, reducing total income to $14,700. With expenses at $14,500, cash flow is nearly zero, and DSCR is approximately 1.01. While the properties are still covering their debt, there is no margin for error.

To mitigate these risks, Lucas maintains six months of reserves for each property. His duplex requires $27,000 in reserves, and his fourplex requires $54,000, for a total of

$81,000. This allows him to cover expenses even in challenging conditions.

Lucas also implements a hybrid rental strategy, converting one unit in the duplex to a long-term rental generating $1,800 per month. This provides a stable income base, reducing the impact of short-term rental fluctuations. After implementing this strategy, his adjusted income in a downturn scenario increases slightly, improving stability. He also reduces expenses by optimizing operations, lowering costs by $500 per month.

Through this analysis, Lucas gains a clear understanding of his risk exposure and takes proactive steps to strengthen his portfolio. By stress testing different scenarios and implementing strategies to mitigate risk, he ensures that his investments remain stable even under challenging conditions.

This example highlights the importance of preparing for uncertainty. By understanding how your portfolio performs under different conditions, you can make informed decisions that protect your income and long-term success.

Chapter 8

Exit Strategies and Wealth Creation with Multi-Unit Airbnb Properties

As you build and scale a portfolio of multi-unit Airbnb properties, one of the most important yet often overlooked components of long-term success is the exit strategy. Many investors focus heavily on acquisition and cash flow, but true wealth is created through intentional exits, strategic repositioning, and the ability to convert equity into new opportunities. An exit strategy is not something you think about at the end—it is something you plan from the very beginning.

Multi-unit Airbnb properties offer a wide range of exit options, far more than most investors realize. Because these properties sit at the intersection of residential and income-producing assets, they can be sold, refinanced, repositioned, or even converted into entirely different investment vehicles. Understanding these options allows you to maximize your returns and maintain flexibility as market conditions change.

The most common exit strategy is selling the property. However, selling is not just about timing the market—it is about positioning the property in a way that maximizes its value. For multi-unit Airbnb properties, this often means demonstrating strong and consistent income performance. A property that is well-documented, professionally managed, and generating reliable income can attract a premium price, especially from investors looking for turnkey opportunities.

Another powerful exit strategy is refinancing. Instead of selling the property, you can refinance to access the equity you have built. This allows you to pull out cash while still retaining ownership and continuing to generate income. In many cases, refinancing can provide enough capital to acquire additional properties, effectively allowing your existing assets to fund your growth. This is one of the key mechanisms behind portfolio scaling.

Cash-out refinancing is particularly effective for multi-unit Airbnb properties because their income potential can significantly increase their value. By improving operations, increasing occupancy, and optimizing pricing, you can raise the property's net income, which can lead to a higher appraisal. This increased value can then be leveraged through refinancing, creating a cycle of growth and reinvestment.

Another advanced exit strategy is converting the property's use. For example, a multi-unit Airbnb property can be transitioned into long-term rentals, mid-term rentals, or even sold as individual units if zoning and legal structures allow. This flexibility provides a hedge against regulatory changes or market shifts. If short-term rental regulations become more restrictive, you can adapt your strategy rather than being forced to exit at a disadvantage.

Portfolio-level exits are also an important consideration. As you accumulate multiple properties, you may choose to sell them as a portfolio rather than individually. This can attract institutional buyers or larger investors who are willing to pay a premium for a stabilized, income-producing portfolio. Portfolio sales can also simplify the exit process and provide a significant liquidity event.

1031 exchanges are another powerful tool for wealth creation. This strategy allows you to sell a property and reinvest the proceeds into another property without immediately paying capital gains taxes. By deferring taxes, you can preserve more capital and continue to grow your portfolio. Multi-unit Airbnb properties are particularly well-suited for this strategy, as they can be exchanged for larger or more valuable assets.

Timing plays a critical role in exit strategies. Market conditions, interest rates, and demand for short-term rentals all influence the optimal time to sell or refinance. While it is impossible to predict the market perfectly, understanding trends and maintaining flexibility allows you to make informed decisions. The goal is not to time the market perfectly, but to position yourself to take advantage of favorable conditions.

Another key factor is property condition and presentation. A well-maintained, professionally managed property with strong financial records is far more attractive to buyers and lenders. Keeping detailed records of income, expenses, and performance not only helps you manage your property but also enhances its value when it is time to exit.

Debt structure also impacts your exit options. Properties with favorable loan terms are easier to refinance or sell, while those with high interest rates or restrictive terms may limit your flexibility. As you structure your deals, consider how your financing will affect your future exit strategies.

Wealth creation in multi-unit Airbnb investing is not just about income—it is about equity growth and leverage. As your properties appreciate in value and generate income, your net worth increases. By strategically accessing this equity and reinvesting it, you create a compounding effect that accelerates wealth creation.

Another advanced concept is creating passive income streams through partial exits. For example, you might sell a portion of your portfolio while retaining your highest-performing properties. This allows you to realize gains while maintaining ongoing income. Alternatively, you might bring in partners or investors, selling a share of the property while retaining control and a portion of the income.

Legacy planning is also an important consideration. Multi-unit properties can be structured in a way that allows them to be passed on to future generations, providing long-term income and financial security. This involves legal and tax planning, but it can transform your portfolio into a lasting asset.

Ultimately, exit strategies are about control and flexibility. They give you the ability to adapt, capitalize on opportunities, and protect your investments. Without a clear exit strategy, even a high-performing property can become a limitation rather than an asset.

This chapter is designed to shift your perspective from simply owning properties to managing them as part of a larger financial strategy. By understanding and planning your exits, you can maximize your returns, reduce risk, and create a pathway to long-term wealth.

Real-Life Math Example: Exit Strategy and Equity Growth in a Multi-Unit Portfolio

Consider an investor named Natalie who owns a triplex purchased for $700,000. She put 25 percent down, investing $175,000, and financed the remaining $525,000. Over three years, she optimized the property, increasing its monthly income from $9,000 to $12,000. Expenses remain at $7,000 per month, resulting in $5,000 in monthly cash flow.

Due to the increased income and market appreciation, the property is now valued at $950,000. Natalie considers two exit strategies: selling or refinancing.

If she sells the property for $950,000, she pays off the remaining loan balance, which has been reduced to approximately $500,000. After selling costs of 6 percent ($57,000), her net proceeds are $393,000. Subtracting her initial investment of $175,000, she realizes a profit of $218,000, in addition to the cash flow she earned during ownership.

Alternatively, Natalie considers a cash-out refinance at 75 percent loan-to-value. This results in a new loan of $712,500. After paying off the existing loan of $500,000, she receives $212,500 in cash. Her new monthly payment increases slightly due to the larger loan, rising to $5,200.

With income remaining at $12,000 and expenses increasing to $7,200 due to the higher mortgage, her new cash flow is $4,800 per month. While slightly lower than before, she now has over $200,000 in capital to invest in another property. Natalie uses this capital to purchase a fourplex for $800,000, putting 25 percent down ($200,000). The new property generates $13,000 in monthly income with $8,500 in expenses, producing $4,500 in cash flow.

Now Natalie owns two properties generating a combined cash flow of $9,300 per month. Over time, she continues to optimize and potentially refinance again, further expanding her portfolio.

This example illustrates the power of strategic exits. By choosing to refinance instead of sell, Natalie retains her original property, continues to generate income, and acquires an additional asset. This creates a compounding effect that accelerates her wealth creation.

Understanding how to evaluate and execute exit strategies allows you to make decisions that align with your long-term goals. Whether you choose to sell, refinance, or reposition your properties, the key is to approach each decision strategically, maximizing both income and equity growth over time.

Chapter 9

Building a Long-Term Legacy with Multi-Unit Airbnb Investing

At some point in your journey, your focus begins to shift. What starts as a strategy to generate income and achieve financial independence evolves into something much larger—a system for creating long-term wealth, stability, and legacy. Multi-unit Airbnb investing is not just about cash flow or scaling a portfolio. When approached correctly, it becomes a vehicle for building generational wealth, creating opportunities for your family, and establishing a financial foundation that can last far beyond your lifetime.

The concept of legacy investing requires a different mindset. It is no longer just about acquiring the next property or increasing monthly income. It is about sustainability, durability, and intentional design. Every decision—from how you finance your properties to how you structure ownership—should be aligned with long-term goals. Multi-unit properties are uniquely positioned for this purpose because they combine strong income potential with scalability and flexibility.

One of the most important aspects of legacy building is ownership structure. Holding properties in the right legal entities can provide liability protection, tax advantages, and ease of transfer. Many investors transition from holding properties in their personal name to using limited liability companies or other structures as their portfolio grows. This not only protects personal assets but also creates a framework for managing and transferring properties more efficiently.

Another key element is consistency of income. Multi-unit Airbnb properties provide multiple income streams within a single asset, which increases stability. Even if one unit experiences lower occupancy, the others can continue to generate revenue. Over time, this consistency becomes the foundation of a reliable income stream that can support your lifestyle and provide security for your family.

Debt strategy also plays a role in legacy building. While leverage is a powerful tool for growth, long-term wealth often involves gradually reducing debt and increasing equity. Some investors choose to pay down their loans over time, eventually owning properties free and clear. Others maintain strategic leverage while ensuring that their properties generate strong cash flow. The key is to balance growth with long-term stability.

Portfolio design is another critical factor. Instead of focusing solely on growth, legacy investors think about how their portfolio will perform over decades. This includes diversifying across markets, property types, and rental strategies. It also involves maintaining a mix of high-growth properties and stable, income-producing assets. This balance ensures that the portfolio can adapt to changing conditions while continuing to generate income.

Succession planning is an essential component of legacy investing. Without a clear plan, even a successful portfolio can become difficult to manage or transfer. This includes determining how properties will be passed on, who will manage them, and how decisions will be made. Clear documentation, legal structures, and communication are key to ensuring a smooth transition.

Education is another powerful tool for building legacy. Teaching the next generation how to manage, operate, and grow the portfolio ensures that the wealth you create is sustained. This includes not only financial education but also operational knowledge—how to manage properties, analyze deals, and make strategic decisions.

Tax strategy becomes increasingly important as your portfolio grows. Understanding how to optimize deductions, manage depreciation, and structure transactions can significantly impact your long-term returns. Working with experienced professionals allows you to maximize efficiency and preserve more of your wealth.

Another important concept is resilience. Markets change, regulations evolve, and unexpected challenges arise. A legacy portfolio must be able to withstand these changes. This means maintaining reserves, avoiding over-leverage, and continuously adapting your strategy. Resilience is what allows your portfolio to endure over time.

Philanthropy and impact are also considerations for many legacy investors. Multi-unit Airbnb properties can create opportunities not only for financial gain but also for community impact. This might include providing quality housing, supporting local economies, or reinvesting in communities. Aligning your investments with your values can add another layer of meaning to your work.

Technology and systems continue to play a role in long-term success. As your portfolio grows, efficient management becomes essential. Automation, data analysis, and standardized processes allow you to maintain performance while reducing complexity. These systems also make it easier to transition management to others in the future.

Another advanced concept is creating passive structures within your portfolio. This might involve hiring property managers, building a team, or creating systems that allow the portfolio to operate with minimal day-to-day involvement. The goal is to create a business that runs efficiently without requiring constant attention.

Equity growth remains a central component of legacy building. As properties appreciate and generate income, your net worth increases. By holding assets over the long term, you benefit from compounding growth. This is one of the most powerful aspects of real estate investing—the ability to build wealth steadily over time.

Flexibility is also important. A legacy portfolio should not be rigid. It should allow for adjustments, whether that means selling underperforming properties, reinvesting in new opportunities, or adapting to changing market conditions. This flexibility ensures that your portfolio remains aligned with your goals.

Ultimately, building a legacy with multi-unit Airbnb investing is about intention. It is about designing a portfolio that not only generates income today but continues to provide value for years to come. It is about creating a system that supports your life and the lives of those who come after you.

This chapter is meant to expand your vision. It is not just about the next deal or the next year—it is about the long term. By applying these principles, you can transform your portfolio into something far greater than a collection of properties. You can create a lasting legacy.

Real-Life Math Example: Long-Term Wealth and Legacy Portfolio Growth

Consider an investor named Victor who begins with a single duplex purchased for $500,000. He puts 20 percent down, investing $100,000, and finances the remaining $400,000. The property generates $5,500 per month in income with $3,500 in expenses, producing $2,000 in monthly cash flow.

Over five years, Victor acquires additional properties using a combination of savings, refinancing, and reinvestment. He now owns three properties: a duplex, a triplex, and a fourplex.

The duplex generates $6,000 per month with $3,800 in expenses, producing $2,200 in cash flow. The triplex generates $9,500 per month with $6,000 in expenses, producing $3,500 in cash flow. The fourplex generates $14,000 per month with $9,000 in expenses, producing $5,000 in cash flow.

Combined, Victor's portfolio generates $29,500 in monthly income and $18,800 in expenses, resulting in $10,700 in monthly cash flow. Annually, this equals $128,400.

Over time, property values increase. The duplex is now worth $650,000, the triplex $900,000, and the fourplex $1,200,000. The total portfolio value is $2,750,000. Loan balances have been reduced to a combined $1,800,000, resulting in $950,000 in equity.

Victor decides to implement a long-term strategy. He allocates a portion of his cash flow to paying down debt, reducing his loan balances over time. He also maintains reserves equal to six months of expenses, totaling approximately $112,800.

After ten years, Victor's properties are largely paid down, and his monthly expenses decrease significantly. His portfolio now generates over $20,000 per month in net income, much of it passive.

Victor then begins planning for succession. He structures his properties within a legal entity and creates a plan for transferring ownership to his children. He also educates them on managing the properties, ensuring that the portfolio continues to perform.

This example demonstrates how multi-unit Airbnb investing can evolve from a single property into a long-term wealth-building system. By focusing on growth, stability, and planning, Victor transforms his investments into a legacy that provides ongoing income and opportunity. The key takeaway is that legacy is built over time through consistent, intentional actions. By thinking long-term and making strategic decisions, you can create a portfolio that not only supports your goals but endures for generations.

Chapter 10

Advanced Airbnb Mortgage Loan Structuring for Maximum Flexibility and Control

At the highest level of multi-unit Airbnb investing, success is no longer defined by simply acquiring properties or generating strong cash flow. It is defined by your ability to structure deals in a way that gives you maximum flexibility, control, and long-term advantage. Advanced loan structuring is where experienced investors separate themselves from the rest. It is not about following standard loan guidelines—it is about strategically combining multiple financing methods to create opportunities that others cannot access.

The modern lending landscape offers a wide range of tools, including DSCR loans, asset-based loans, portfolio loans, seller financing, and creative structures. Each of these options has its own strengths, and when used together, they can unlock deals that would otherwise be impossible. The key is understanding how to layer these tools in a way that aligns with your investment strategy.

One of the most powerful concepts in advanced structuring is flexibility. Traditional financing often comes with rigid guidelines, but alternative lending products provide more room to adapt. For example, DSCR loans allow you to qualify based on property income rather than personal income, while asset-based loans focus on your overall financial strength. By combining these approaches, you can structure deals that fit your unique situation.

Another important concept is control. Maintaining control over your properties and your financing is essential for long-term success. This includes choosing loan terms that align with your goals, avoiding restrictive covenants, and ensuring that you have the ability to refinance or reposition your properties when needed. Control also means having multiple options—so you are not dependent on a single lender or strategy.

Layering financing is a key strategy in advanced structuring. This involves using multiple sources of capital within a single deal. For example, you might use a primary loan to cover the majority of the purchase price, a secondary loan or line of credit to cover part of the down payment, and your own capital for the remainder. This approach allows you to leverage your resources more effectively and preserve capital for future investments.

Seller financing is another powerful tool. In some cases, the seller may be willing to finance a portion of the purchase price, reducing the need for traditional financing. This can be particularly useful in competitive markets or for properties that do not fit standard lending criteria. Seller financing can also provide more flexible terms, such as lower interest rates or deferred payments.

Bridge loans are often used in advanced structuring to facilitate acquisitions or transitions. These short-term loans provide immediate capital, allowing you to acquire a property quickly and then refinance into a long-term loan once the property is stabilized. This is particularly useful for properties that require improvements or repositioning before they can qualify for traditional financing.

Another advanced strategy is cross-collateralization, where multiple properties are used as collateral for a single loan. This can increase your borrowing capacity and allow you to access larger amounts of capital. However, it also introduces additional risk, as multiple properties are tied to the same loan. Understanding when and how to use this strategy is critical.

Interest-only loans are another tool that can improve cash flow in the short term. By reducing your monthly payments, you can increase your cash flow and reinvest more capital into your portfolio. However, these loans do not reduce your principal, so they must be used strategically and with a clear plan for the future. Another key concept is timing. Advanced structuring often involves multiple steps, such as acquiring a property, improving it, and then refinancing. Each step must be carefully timed to maximize value and minimize risk. This requires a clear understanding of market conditions, lender requirements, and your own financial position.

Documentation and presentation also become more important at this level. When working with alternative lenders or structuring complex deals, you must be able to clearly demonstrate the strength of your investment. This includes detailed financial projections, market analysis, and a well-defined strategy. The more prepared you are, the more options you will have.

Risk management remains a central consideration. While advanced structuring can increase your opportunities, it can also introduce complexity. Each additional layer of financing adds another variable that must be managed. Maintaining reserves, monitoring performance, and staying organized are essential to managing this complexity.

Another advanced concept is creating optionality. This means structuring your deals in a way that gives you multiple paths forward. For example, you might structure a property so that it can be operated as a short-term rental, long-term rental, or sold as individual units. This flexibility allows you to adapt to changing conditions and capitalize on opportunities.

Portfolio-level structuring is the next step. Instead of focusing on individual deals, you begin to structure your entire portfolio strategically. This includes balancing different types of loans, managing overall leverage, and aligning your financing with your long-term goals. This holistic approach allows you to optimize performance across your entire portfolio.

As you reach this level, relationships become increasingly important. Working with experienced lenders, brokers, and advisors can provide access to opportunities and insights that are not available to the general market. Building these relationships is an investment in your future success.

Ultimately, advanced loan structuring is about creating a system that works for you. It is about using every available tool to maximize your potential while maintaining control and managing risk. When done correctly, it allows you to operate at a level where opportunities are no longer limited by standard guidelines.

This chapter represents the culmination of everything you

have learned in this series. It is about taking your knowledge and applying it in a way that creates true leverage—not just financial, but strategic. By mastering advanced structuring, you position yourself to operate at the highest level of multi-unit Airbnb investing.

Real-Life Math Example: Layering Financing for a Fourplex Airbnb Deal

Consider an investor named Daniel who is acquiring a fourplex priced at $1,000,000. Instead of using a traditional 25 percent down payment entirely from his own funds, he structures the deal using multiple financing sources.

Daniel secures a primary DSCR loan covering 70 percent of the purchase price, or $700,000. The loan has an interest rate of 7.5 percent, resulting in a monthly payment of approximately $4,900. To cover part of the remaining 30 percent, Daniel uses a home equity line of credit (HELOC) to finance $150,000 at an interest rate of 8 percent, with a monthly payment of approximately $1,000. He contributes $150,000 of his own capital to complete the purchase.

The property generates $16,000 per month in short-term rental income. Operating expenses, including taxes, insurance, utilities, and maintenance, total $6,000 per month. Combined loan payments are $4,900 (DSCR loan) + $1,000 (HELOC), totaling $5,900.

Total monthly expenses are $6,000 (operations) + $5,900 (debt), which equals $11,900. Subtracting this from income of $16,000 results in $4,100 in monthly cash flow. Daniel calculates DSCR based on the primary loan. Dividing income of $16,000 by total expenses of $11,900 results in a DSCR of approximately 1.34, meeting lender requirements.

After one year of optimization, Daniel increases income to $18,000 per month. Expenses remain at $11,900, increasing cash flow to $6,100 per month. The property is reappraised at $1,200,000 due to its improved performance.

Daniel refinances the property at 75 percent loan-to-value, resulting in a new loan of $900,000. He pays off the original DSCR loan and the HELOC, totaling $850,000, and receives $50,000 in additional cash.

His new loan has a monthly payment of approximately $6,300. With income at $18,000 and operating expenses at $6,000, total expenses are $12,300, resulting in $5,700 in monthly cash flow.

Through this structure, Daniel was able to acquire the property with less personal capital, increase its performance, and then refinance into a simpler, more stable loan. He also freed up capital to pursue additional investments.

This example demonstrates how advanced structuring can create opportunities that are not possible with traditional approaches. By layering financing and planning for future steps, Daniel maximizes both his immediate returns and his long-term growth potential.

When applied strategically, these techniques allow you to operate at a higher level, turning complex deals into powerful wealth-building opportunities.

Chapter 11

Creating Systems, Automation, and Operational Excellence for Multi-Unit Airbnb Portfolios

As your multi-unit Airbnb portfolio grows, the greatest threat to your success is no longer finding deals or securing financing—it is operational complexity. What works for one property quickly becomes overwhelming across multiple units, buildings, and markets. This is where systems, automation, and operational excellence become the foundation of sustainable success. Without them, growth creates chaos. With them, growth becomes scalable, predictable, and highly profitable.

At its core, operational excellence is about consistency. Every guest, every unit, and every interaction should deliver a reliable and high-quality experience. In multi-unit properties, this is even more important because one breakdown can affect multiple guests at the same time. Systems ensure that nothing is left to chance, and automation ensures that those systems run efficiently without constant manual oversight.

The first step in building operational systems is standardization. This means creating repeatable processes for every aspect of your business—guest communication, booking management, cleaning, maintenance, pricing, and financial tracking. Instead of reinventing the process for each property, you develop a blueprint that can be applied across your entire portfolio. This reduces errors, saves time, and improves performance.

Guest communication is one of the most critical areas to systematize. Timely and professional communication directly impacts reviews, bookings, and overall guest satisfaction. Automated messaging systems can handle inquiries, confirmations, check-in instructions, and follow-ups, ensuring that every guest receives consistent and prompt communication. This not only improves efficiency but also enhances the guest experience.

Cleaning and turnover management are equally important. In multi-unit properties, coordinating cleanings across multiple units can become complex. Standardized cleaning checklists, scheduled workflows, and reliable cleaning teams ensure that each unit is prepared to the same standard every time. Automation tools can help schedule cleanings based on bookings, reducing the risk of missed or delayed turnovers.

Maintenance systems are another key component. Proactive maintenance prevents small issues from becoming costly problems. This includes regular inspections, tracking repairs, and maintaining a list of trusted vendors. Having a system in place allows you to address issues quickly and minimize disruptions to your guests.

Dynamic pricing and revenue management can also be automated. Pricing tools analyze market data, demand trends, and competition to adjust your rates in real time. This ensures that you are maximizing revenue without constantly monitoring the market. In multi-unit properties, this can significantly increase income while reducing the time required to manage pricing manually.

Financial tracking and reporting are essential for understanding performance. Systems should be in place to track income, expenses, and key metrics such as occupancy, average daily rate, and cash flow. This data allows you to make informed decisions and identify areas for improvement. Automation can simplify this process, providing real-time insights into your portfolio's performance.

Another important aspect of operational excellence is team building. As your portfolio grows, it becomes difficult to manage everything on your own. Building a reliable team, whether in-house or outsourced, allows you to delegate tasks and focus on higher-level strategy. This includes cleaners, maintenance personnel, property managers, and administrative support. Training and accountability are critical when working with a team. Clear expectations, standardized procedures, and regular communication ensure that everyone is aligned. Performance metrics and feedback systems help maintain quality and identify areas for improvement. A strong team is one of the most valuable assets in scaling your portfolio.

Technology integration is what ties all these systems together. Property management software can centralize bookings, communication, and operations. Automation tools can handle repetitive tasks, while data analytics provide insights into performance. By integrating these tools, you create a seamless workflow that reduces complexity and increases efficiency.

Another advanced concept is creating redundancy within your systems. This means having backup plans in place for critical operations. For example, having multiple cleaning teams or backup vendors ensures that your operations continue even if one resource becomes unavailable. Redundancy reduces risk and increases reliability.

Time management is also transformed through systems and automation. Instead of being involved in every detail, you can focus on strategic decisions, such as acquiring new properties, optimizing performance, and expanding your portfolio. This shift from operator to strategist is a key milestone in your journey.

Scalability is the ultimate goal of operational excellence. A well-designed system allows you to add new properties without significantly increasing your workload. Each new unit becomes an extension of your existing framework rather than a new challenge. This is what enables rapid and sustainable growth.

Another important aspect is guest experience consistency. Regardless of which unit a guest stays in, they should receive the same level of quality and service. This builds your brand, increases repeat bookings, and strengthens your reputation. Consistency is what turns a collection of properties into a recognizable and trusted business.

Operational excellence also improves profitability. By reducing inefficiencies, minimizing errors, and optimizing processes, you increase your net income. Small improvements in operations can lead to significant financial gains over time, especially across multiple units.

As your portfolio matures, you may choose to transition into a more passive role. With strong systems and a reliable team in place, your involvement can be reduced to oversight and strategic planning. This allows you to enjoy the benefits of your investments without being tied to day-to-day operations. Ultimately, systems and automation are not just tools—they are the foundation of long-term success. They allow you to scale, maintain quality, and maximize profitability while reducing stress and complexity. Investors who master this aspect of the business are able to operate at a level that others cannot sustain.

This chapter is about building that foundation. By implementing these principles, you create a business that is not only profitable but also efficient, scalable, and resilient.

Real-Life Math Example: Increasing Profit Through Operational Efficiency

Consider an investor named Olivia who owns a fourplex Airbnb property generating $16,000 per month in gross income. Her operating expenses, including cleaning, maintenance, utilities, and management inefficiencies, total $7,000 per month. Her mortgage, taxes, and insurance add another $6,000, bringing total expenses to $13,000. This results in a monthly cash flow of $3,000.

Olivia notices that her operations are inconsistent. Cleaning costs vary, maintenance issues are reactive rather than proactive, and pricing is not optimized. She decides to implement systems and automation.

First, Olivia standardizes her cleaning process and negotiates a contract with a cleaning company, reducing cleaning costs by $800 per month. She also implements a maintenance schedule, reducing unexpected repairs by $400 per month. Utilities are optimized through energy-efficient upgrades, saving another $300 per month.

Next, Olivia implements dynamic pricing software, increasing her monthly income from $16,000 to $17,500. She also improves guest communication and listing quality, increasing occupancy slightly.

After these changes, Olivia's new monthly income is $17,500. Her operating expenses are reduced to $5,500, and her fixed costs remain at $6,000. Total expenses are now $11,500.

Her new monthly cash flow is $17,500 minus $11,500, which equals $6,000. This is a $3,000 increase in cash flow, effectively doubling her profit without acquiring a new property.

Annually, her cash flow increases from $36,000 to $72,000. This improvement also increases her property's value, as higher income can support a higher valuation.

Olivia also calculates her DSCR. Previously, her ratio was $16,000 divided by $13,000, or approximately 1.23. After optimization, her DSCR is $17,500 divided by $11,500, or approximately 1.52. This stronger ratio improves her ability to refinance or acquire additional properties. This example demonstrates how operational excellence can significantly impact financial performance. By focusing on systems, automation, and efficiency, Olivia transforms her property into a high-performing asset.

The key takeaway is that growth does not always require new acquisitions. Sometimes, the greatest gains come from improving what you already have. By applying these principles across your portfolio, you can increase income, reduce costs, and create a business that is both scalable and sustainable.

Chapter 12

The Complete Blueprint for Dominating Multi-Unit Airbnb Investing

By the time you reach this stage, you are no longer just learning how to invest—you are building a system that can consistently produce results. This final chapter brings everything together into a complete blueprint for dominating the multi-unit Airbnb space. It is about integrating financing, deal structuring, underwriting, operations, scaling, risk management, and exit strategies into one unified approach that allows you to operate at a high level with clarity and confidence.

The first pillar of this blueprint is clarity of strategy. Every successful investor operates with a defined approach. You must know what type of properties you are targeting, what markets you are focusing on, what loan products you will use, and what your income goals are. Without this clarity, you risk making inconsistent decisions that slow your progress. With it, every action becomes intentional and aligned with your long-term vision.

The second pillar is deal acquisition. Finding the right deals is not about volume—it is about precision. You are looking for properties that meet specific criteria, including strong income potential, favorable zoning, and alignment with your financing strategy. Multi-unit properties provide a unique advantage because they allow you to generate multiple income streams from a single acquisition. However, this also means that your analysis must be thorough and data-driven.

The third pillar is financing mastery. Understanding how to use different loan products—such as DSCR loans, conventional loans, and creative financing—gives you the ability to structure deals in a way that maximizes leverage and flexibility. Financing is not just a requirement; it is a tool. The more you understand it, the more opportunities you can access.

The fourth pillar is operational excellence. As discussed in previous chapters, systems and automation are essential for managing multi-unit properties effectively. Without them, scaling becomes difficult and inconsistent. With them, you create a business that can grow without increasing complexity at the same rate.

The fifth pillar is income optimization. Revenue is not static. Through dynamic pricing, improved guest experience, and strategic positioning, you can continuously increase your income. At the same time, controlling expenses ensures that your growth translates into higher profits. The sixth pillar is scaling. Once you have a system that works, the next step is to replicate it. Scaling is about repeating successful processes, leveraging financing, and reinvesting profits. It is not about rushing—it is about building momentum in a controlled and sustainable way.

The seventh pillar is risk management. Growth without stability is fragile. By maintaining reserves, diversifying your portfolio, and preparing for different scenarios, you create a foundation that can withstand challenges. This allows you to continue growing even in uncertain conditions.

The eighth pillar is exit strategy. Every property should have a clear plan for the future. Whether you choose to refinance, sell, or reposition, your exit strategy should align with your overall goals. This ensures that your portfolio remains flexible and adaptable.

The ninth pillar is mindset. Success in multi-unit Airbnb investing requires discipline, patience, and a willingness to learn. There will be challenges, but each one provides an opportunity to improve your system. The most successful investors are those who remain consistent and focused over time.

When these pillars are combined, they create a powerful framework. You are no longer reacting to opportunities—you are creating them. You are not just managing properties—you are building a business. This shift in perspective is what allows you to dominate the market.

Another important aspect of this blueprint is continuous improvement. Markets evolve, technologies advance, and guest expectations change. Staying ahead requires a commitment to learning and adapting. This might involve testing new pricing strategies, exploring new markets, or adopting new tools. The goal is to remain competitive and innovative.

Collaboration and networking also play a role. Building relationships with lenders, brokers, contractors, and other investors can provide access to opportunities and insights that are not available otherwise. These connections can accelerate your growth and help you navigate challenges more effectively.

Portfolio management becomes increasingly important as you grow. Instead of focusing on individual properties, you begin to manage your portfolio as a whole. This includes balancing risk and return, optimizing performance across properties, and making strategic decisions about acquisitions and exits.

Another advanced concept is creating a brand. As you operate multiple units, especially within the same market, you can develop a recognizable identity. This can improve guest trust, increase repeat bookings, and differentiate your properties from competitors. Branding turns your portfolio into more than just a collection of properties—it becomes a business with a reputation.

Financial discipline remains at the core of everything. Tracking performance, maintaining reserves, and making data-driven decisions ensure that your growth is sustainable. This discipline is what allows you to scale without losing control.

As you implement this blueprint, you will begin to see results compound. Each property adds to your income, each improvement increases your efficiency, and each strategic decision strengthens your position. Over time, this creates a portfolio that generates significant income and long-term wealth.

Ultimately, dominating multi-unit Airbnb investing is not about a single strategy or tactic. It is about integrating multiple elements into a cohesive system. It is about thinking strategically, acting consistently, and continuously improving.

This chapter is your roadmap. It is the culmination of everything you have learned, designed to guide you toward mastery. By following this blueprint, you can build a portfolio that not only performs but excels, creating opportunities and wealth for years to come.

Real-Life Math Example: Building a Complete Multi-Unit Airbnb Portfolio System

Consider an investor named Adrian who follows this blueprint to build his portfolio. He begins with a duplex purchased for $550,000, putting 20 percent down ($110,000). The property generates $6,500 per month in income with $4,000 in expenses, producing $2,500 in monthly cash flow.

Using this cash flow and additional savings, Adrian acquires a triplex for $750,000 with a 25 percent down payment ($187,500). This property generates $10,500 per month with $6,800 in expenses, producing $3,700 in cash flow.

After optimizing both properties, Adrian refinances the duplex, pulling out $80,000 in equity. He combines this with savings to acquire a fourplex for $1,000,000, putting $250,000 down. The fourplex generates $15,000 per month with $9,500 in expenses, producing $5,500 in cash flow.

At this stage, Adrian's portfolio includes three properties generating a combined monthly income of $32,000 and expenses of $20,300, resulting in $11,700 in cash flow.

Adrian then implements operational systems, increasing efficiency and reducing expenses by $1,000 per month across the portfolio. He also improves pricing and guest experience, increasing income by $2,000 per month. His updated numbers are $34,000 in income and $19,300 in expenses, resulting in $14,700 in monthly cash flow. Annually, this equals $176,400.

Adrian maintains reserves equal to six months of expenses, totaling approximately $115,800. He also diversifies his portfolio by acquiring properties in different markets over time.

After several years, Adrian's portfolio grows to five properties, generating over $25,000 per month in cash flow. Property values have appreciated, and his equity exceeds $1.5 million.

Adrian now has multiple options. He can continue scaling, refinance to access capital, or begin selling properties strategically to realize gains. He also structures his portfolio for long-term stability and potential transfer to future generations.

This example demonstrates how the blueprint works in practice. By combining acquisition, financing, optimization, and scaling, Adrian builds a system that generates consistent income and long-term wealth.

The key takeaway is that success is not based on a single deal—it is built through a system. By following this blueprint, you can create a portfolio that grows, performs, and adapts over time, allowing you to achieve your financial goals and beyond.

Chapter 13

The Future of Multi-Unit Airbnb Investing and Staying Ahead of the Market

As you reach this stage, you are no longer simply participating in the multi-unit Airbnb market—you are positioned to anticipate where it is going. The investors who dominate this space over the next decade will not just follow trends; they will understand them early, adapt quickly, and structure their portfolios to benefit from change. The future of multi-unit Airbnb investing will be shaped by technology, regulation, evolving guest expectations, and shifting financial markets. Your ability to stay ahead of these forces will determine your long-term success.

One of the most important trends shaping the future is the increasing professionalization of the short-term rental industry. What began as a casual side income opportunity has evolved into a highly competitive business environment. Multi-unit properties are at the center of this shift because they allow operators to run their investments more like hospitality businesses. This means higher standards, better systems, and more strategic management. Investors who treat their properties as businesses rather than passive assets will have a significant advantage.

Technology will continue to transform every aspect of the business. Dynamic pricing tools, automation platforms, and data analytics are already becoming standard, but their capabilities will expand. Advanced algorithms will allow for more precise pricing, better demand forecasting, and improved operational efficiency. Investors who embrace these tools will be able to optimize performance in ways that were not possible before. At the same time, technology will lower barriers to entry, increasing competition and making it even more important to differentiate your properties.

Guest expectations are also evolving. Travelers are no longer just looking for a place to stay—they are seeking experiences. This includes design, amenities, convenience, and personalized service. Multi-unit properties provide an opportunity to create consistent, high-quality experiences across multiple units, building a brand that guests recognize and trust. Investors who focus on guest experience will be able to command higher rates and maintain stronger occupancy.

Regulation will remain a key factor in the future of Airbnb investing. As cities and governments continue to adapt to the growth of short-term rentals, new rules and restrictions are likely to emerge. Multi-unit properties may face increased scrutiny, particularly in densely populated areas. Staying informed and adaptable will be essential. This includes understanding local laws, maintaining compliance, and being prepared to adjust your strategy if needed.

Another important trend is the rise of hybrid rental models. The line between short-term, mid-term, and long-term rentals is becoming increasingly blurred. Investors are combining these strategies to create more stable and flexible income streams. For example, during slower seasons, units can be rented for longer stays, while peak periods can focus on short-term bookings. This adaptability reduces risk and improves overall performance.

Financing will also continue to evolve. As lenders become more familiar with short-term rental income, new loan products and underwriting methods are likely to emerge. This could include more widespread acceptance of short-term rental data, improved DSCR models, and greater flexibility for investors. Staying informed about these developments allows you to take advantage of new opportunities as they arise.

Market selection will become even more critical. As competition increases, not all markets will perform equally. Identifying emerging markets with strong demand, favorable regulations, and growth potential will be key to staying ahead. This requires ongoing research and a willingness to explore new opportunities rather than relying solely on established locations.

Another trend is the consolidation of portfolios. As the industry matures, larger investors and institutions may begin to acquire multi-unit Airbnb properties at scale. This creates both competition and opportunity. While competition may increase in some markets, there may also be opportunities to sell properties or portfolios at premium prices to institutional buyers.

Sustainability and environmental considerations are also becoming more important. Guests are increasingly aware of energy usage, waste, and environmental impact. Implementing sustainable practices, such as energy-efficient systems and eco-friendly amenities, can not only reduce costs but also attract a growing segment of environmentally conscious travelers.

Branding will play a larger role in the future. As more investors enter the market, differentiation becomes essential. Creating a recognizable brand across your properties can improve guest loyalty, increase repeat bookings, and provide a competitive edge. Multi-unit properties are particularly well-suited for branding because they allow for consistency and scale within a single location.

Another advanced concept is data-driven decision-making. Successful investors will rely increasingly on data to guide their strategies. This includes analyzing market trends, tracking performance metrics, and testing different approaches. Data provides clarity and allows you to make informed decisions rather than relying on assumptions.

Flexibility will remain one of the most important qualities for long-term success. The ability to adapt to changing conditions—whether they are regulatory, economic, or market-driven—ensures that your portfolio remains resilient. This may involve adjusting your rental strategy, exploring new financing options, or repositioning your properties.

As you look to the future, it is important to maintain a long-term perspective. Short-term fluctuations are inevitable, but the overall trend of short-term rental demand remains strong. Multi-unit properties provide a unique opportunity to capture this demand at scale, creating a powerful foundation for growth.

Ultimately, staying ahead of the market is about awareness and action. It is about continuously learning, adapting, and refining your approach. The investors who succeed are those who anticipate change and position themselves accordingly. This chapter is your guide to thinking forward. By understanding the trends shaping the future and preparing for them today, you can build a portfolio that not only survives but thrives in the years to come.

Real-Life Math Example: Adapting a Multi-Unit Portfolio to Future Market Trends

Consider an investor named Sofia who owns a fourplex generating $16,000 per month in short-term rental income with $10,000 in expenses, resulting in $6,000 in monthly cash flow.

Sofia notices increasing competition in her market and a slight decline in occupancy. She decides to adapt her strategy by implementing a hybrid rental model. Two units remain short-term rentals, while the other two are converted to mid-term rentals targeting traveling professionals.

The two short-term units now generate $3,500 each, totaling $7,000. The two mid-term units generate $2,800 each, totaling $5,600. Combined income is $12,600, which is lower than before, but more stable.

Sofia also implements advanced pricing tools and improves her guest experience, increasing short-term rental income slightly. Total income rises to $13,500. At the same time, she reduces expenses through efficiency improvements, lowering total expenses from $10,000 to $9,000. Her new cash flow is $4,500 per month.

While her cash flow is lower than the original $6,000, her income is now more stable and less dependent on seasonal demand. She also experiences fewer vacancies and lower operational stress.

Sofia then evaluates the long-term impact. With more stable income, her DSCR remains strong, allowing her to refinance if needed. She also positions her property to adapt to future regulatory changes, as mid-term rentals are often less restricted.

Over time, Sofia identifies a new market with strong growth potential. Using savings and refinancing, she acquires another multi-unit property, applying her hybrid strategy from the start.

Her combined portfolio now generates $22,000 per month in income with $14,000 in expenses, resulting in $8,000 in cash flow. More importantly, her income is diversified across different rental models and markets.

This example demonstrates how adapting to future trends can strengthen your portfolio. By adjusting her strategy, Sofia reduces risk, maintains profitability, and positions herself for continued growth. The key takeaway is that the future belongs to those who adapt. By staying informed, embracing change, and making strategic decisions, you can ensure that your portfolio remains competitive and successful in an evolving market.

Chapter 14

Becoming the Operator—From Investor to Multi-Unit Airbnb Business Owner

At the highest level of multi-unit Airbnb investing, there is a fundamental shift that takes place. You stop thinking like an investor who owns properties and begin operating like a business owner who controls a scalable hospitality system. This transition is what separates those who earn supplemental income from those who build true financial empires. Multi-unit properties are not just assets—they are operating businesses, and your role evolves from deal finder to operator, strategist, and leader.

In the beginning, most investors focus on acquisition—finding deals, securing financing, and getting properties up and running. While this phase is critical, it is only the starting point. Long-term success depends on your ability to operate efficiently, consistently, and at scale. This requires a different mindset, one that prioritizes systems, performance, and continuous improvement over individual transactions.

The first step in becoming an operator is understanding that your business has multiple layers. At the top level, you have strategy—deciding where to invest, how to finance, and how to grow. At the operational level, you have processes—managing bookings, cleaning, maintenance, and guest communication. At the financial level, you have performance—tracking income, expenses, and profitability. Each of these layers must work together seamlessly.

One of the most important shifts is moving from reactive management to proactive control. Instead of responding to issues as they arise, you build systems that prevent them. This includes standardized procedures, automation tools, and performance monitoring. When your operations are proactive, you reduce errors, improve guest experience, and increase efficiency.

Leadership becomes a central component of your role. As your portfolio grows, you will rely on a team to manage day-to-day operations. This may include cleaners, maintenance staff, property managers, and administrative support. Your responsibility is to ensure that this team operates effectively, follows your systems, and delivers consistent results. Strong leadership creates accountability and drives performance.

Brand building is another key aspect of operating at a higher level. Instead of managing individual listings, you begin to create a cohesive brand across your properties. This includes consistent design, quality standards, and guest experience. A strong brand increases trust, attracts repeat guests, and allows you to command higher rates.

Performance tracking becomes more sophisticated as you transition into an operator role. You are no longer just looking at monthly cash flow—you are analyzing key performance indicators such as occupancy rates, average daily rates, revenue per available unit, and operating margins. These metrics provide insights into how your properties are performing and where improvements can be made.

Another important concept is operational leverage. This refers to your ability to increase income without a proportional increase in effort or cost. Multi-unit properties naturally provide this advantage because multiple units can be managed within the same system. By optimizing your operations, you can increase efficiency and profitability across your entire portfolio.

Time management also changes significantly. Instead of spending time on tasks, you focus on decisions. Your role becomes one of oversight and strategy rather than execution. This allows you to scale your business without being limited by your personal time.

Standardization is critical for maintaining quality as you grow. Every unit should meet the same standards, follow the same processes, and deliver the same level of experience. This consistency is what allows you to scale without sacrificing performance.

Another advanced concept is creating a centralized operation. Instead of managing each property independently, you consolidate your operations into a single system. This includes centralized communication, scheduling, and management. This approach reduces complexity and improves efficiency.

Financial management becomes more strategic as well. You are no longer just tracking income and expenses—you are managing cash flow, planning for future investments, and optimizing your capital. This includes making decisions about refinancing, reinvesting, and allocating resources across your portfolio.

Risk management remains a priority. As an operator, you must ensure that your business can withstand challenges. This includes maintaining reserves, diversifying your portfolio, and continuously monitoring performance. A well-managed operation is more resilient and better positioned for long-term success.

Another important aspect is innovation. The short-term rental market is constantly evolving, and staying competitive requires adapting to new trends and technologies. This might involve adopting new tools, experimenting with different pricing strategies, or enhancing your guest experience. Innovation keeps your business ahead of the competition.

Scaling as an operator requires discipline. It is not just about acquiring more properties—it is about ensuring that your systems can support growth. Each new property should integrate seamlessly into your existing framework. This requires careful planning and execution.

Another key concept is creating value beyond income. As an operator, you are building a business that has intrinsic value. This includes your brand, systems, and performance. A well-run multi-unit Airbnb business can be sold or leveraged in ways that go beyond the value of the individual properties.

Ultimately, becoming an operator is about control and vision. It is about taking ownership of every aspect of your business and aligning it with your long-term goals. This shift in mindset allows you to move from managing properties to building a scalable and sustainable enterprise.

This chapter is designed to guide you through that transition. By adopting an operator mindset and implementing the principles outlined here, you can elevate your business to a level where growth is not just possible but inevitable.

Real-Life Math Example: Transitioning from Investor to Operator

Consider an investor named Marcus who owns two properties: a duplex and a triplex. Initially, he manages both properties manually. The duplex generates $6,000 per month with $3,800 in expenses, producing $2,200 in cash flow. The triplex generates $9,000 per month with $6,200 in expenses, producing $2,800 in cash flow. Combined, Marcus earns $5,000 per month.

However, Marcus spends a significant amount of time managing operations, and his processes are inconsistent. He decides to transition into an operator by implementing systems and building a team.

Marcus hires a cleaning company and negotiates a fixed rate, reducing cleaning costs by $500 per month across both properties. He also implements dynamic pricing, increasing total income by $1,500 per month. Additionally, he introduces automation for guest communication, reducing errors and improving reviews.

After these changes, his duplex income increases to $6,800 with expenses reduced to $3,500, producing $3,300 in cash flow. His triplex income increases to $10,200 with expenses reduced to $5,800, producing $4,400 in cash flow. Combined,

Marcus now earns $7,700 per month, an increase of $2,700 without acquiring new properties.

Marcus then acquires a fourplex using the same systems. The new property generates $14,000 per month with $9,000 in expenses, producing $5,000 in cash flow.

His total portfolio now generates $31,000 in income and $18,300 in expenses, resulting in $12,700 in monthly cash flow.

Because Marcus has systems in place, managing the additional property does not significantly increase his workload. His role shifts to overseeing operations and making strategic decisions.

Over time, Marcus continues to optimize his portfolio, increasing efficiency and profitability. His business becomes more stable, scalable, and valuable.

This example demonstrates the power of transitioning from investor to operator. By focusing on systems, efficiency, and strategy, Marcus significantly increases his income and creates a business that can grow without being limited by his time.

The key takeaway is that success at this level is not about doing more—it is about operating better. By becoming an operator, you unlock the full potential of your multi-unit Airbnb portfolio and position yourself for long-term growth and success.

Chapter 15

Mastery, Freedom, and the Final Evolution of Multi-Unit Airbnb Wealth

At the highest level of multi-unit Airbnb investing, the goal is no longer just income, scaling, or even portfolio size. The ultimate destination is mastery—where your systems run efficiently, your portfolio produces consistent and growing income, and your time is no longer tied to the day-to-day operations of your business. This is where financial freedom, time freedom, and strategic control converge. It is the final evolution from investor, to operator, to architect of a fully optimized wealth system.

Mastery begins with simplification. While earlier stages of growth involve complexity—learning financing, structuring deals, managing operations—the final stage is about refining and streamlining. You begin to eliminate inefficiencies, consolidate systems, and focus only on what produces the highest return. This includes optimizing your portfolio, removing underperforming assets, and doubling down on properties and markets that deliver consistent results.

One of the defining characteristics of mastery is predictability. Your income becomes stable, your systems are reliable, and your operations run smoothly without constant oversight. This predictability is what allows you to step back and enjoy the benefits of your work. It is also what makes your portfolio more valuable, as stability is highly attractive to buyers and investors.

Another key aspect is control over your time. In earlier stages, your time is often consumed by tasks and operations. As you reach mastery, your role shifts almost entirely to strategic decision-making. You are no longer involved in daily management—you are guiding the direction of your business. This allows you to focus on opportunities, innovation, and personal priorities.

Financial freedom is a natural outcome of this stage. With multiple income-producing properties generating consistent cash flow, your reliance on active income disappears. Your portfolio becomes your primary source of income, providing both security and flexibility. This freedom allows you to make decisions based on preference rather than necessity.

Portfolio optimization becomes the primary focus. Instead of acquiring more properties, you refine what you already own. This might involve selling underperforming assets, refinancing to improve cash flow, or upgrading properties to increase income. The goal is to maximize efficiency and return on each asset. Another important concept is income quality. Not all income is equal. High-quality income is stable, predictable, and requires minimal effort to maintain. As you refine your portfolio, you prioritize properties and strategies that produce this type of income. This reduces stress and increases sustainability.

Wealth preservation also becomes a priority. As your net worth grows, protecting your assets is just as important as growing them. This includes legal structures, insurance, diversification, and conservative financial management. The goal is to ensure that your wealth is not only built but maintained over time.

Another advanced concept is creating multiple layers of income. Beyond rental income, your portfolio can generate additional revenue streams, such as management fees, consulting, partnerships, or even selling your systems and expertise. This diversification further strengthens your financial position.

Legacy planning reaches its peak at this stage. You are no longer just building wealth—you are designing how it will be sustained and transferred. This includes structuring your portfolio for succession, educating the next generation, and ensuring that your systems can continue to operate without you.

Another key element of mastery is optionality. You have the ability to choose your path. You can continue to grow, maintain your portfolio, or exit strategically. This flexibility is one of the greatest advantages of reaching this level.

Market awareness remains important, but your perspective changes. Instead of reacting to market changes, you anticipate them. Your experience and systems allow you to adapt quickly and take advantage of opportunities.

Another defining feature of mastery is confidence. You understand your business, your numbers, and your strategy. This confidence allows you to make decisions with clarity and precision. It also allows you to navigate challenges without uncertainty.

At this stage, your business becomes an asset in itself. It is no longer just a collection of properties—it is a system that produces income, operates efficiently, and holds value. This makes it attractive to buyers, investors, and partners.

Exit strategies become more refined. You may choose to sell individual properties, your entire portfolio, or even your business as a whole. Each option provides different benefits, and your decision will depend on your goals and market conditions.

Another important aspect is lifestyle design. With financial and time freedom, you can structure your life in a way that aligns with your priorities. This might include travel, family time, or pursuing other interests. Your business supports your life, rather than the other way around.

Continuous improvement does not stop at mastery. Even at this level, there are always opportunities to refine and optimize. The difference is that these improvements are strategic rather than reactive.

Ultimately, mastery is about alignment. It is about aligning your portfolio, your systems, your finances, and your life in a way that creates harmony and sustainability. It is the culmination of everything you have learned and built.

This chapter represents the final stage of your journey. It is not an end, but a new beginning—one where you operate from a position of strength, clarity, and freedom. By reaching this level, you have created not just a portfolio, but a system of wealth that can support you and your legacy for years to come.

Real-Life Math Example: Achieving Mastery and Financial Freedom

Consider an investor named Daniel who has built a portfolio of five multi-unit Airbnb properties over several years. His portfolio includes two duplexes, one triplex, and two fourplexes.

The first duplex generates $6,500 per month with $4,000 in expenses, producing $2,500 in cash flow. The second duplex generates $7,000 per month with $4,200 in expenses, producing $2,800 in cash flow. The triplex generates $10,500 per month with $6,500 in expenses, producing $4,000 in cash flow. The first fourplex generates $15,000 per month with $9,500 in expenses, producing $5,500 in cash flow. The second fourplex generates $16,000 per month with $10,000 in expenses, producing $6,000 in cash flow.

Combined, Daniel's portfolio generates $55,000 per month in income and $34,200 in expenses, resulting in $20,800 in monthly cash flow. Annually, this equals $249,600.

Daniel decides to optimize his portfolio. He sells one underperforming duplex for $650,000, reducing his workload and reallocating capital. He uses the proceeds to pay down debt on his remaining properties, reducing monthly expenses by $2,000.

After optimization, his portfolio generates $48,000 in income with $30,200 in expenses, resulting in $17,800 in monthly cash flow. While total income is slightly lower, his portfolio is more efficient and easier to manage.

Daniel also implements advanced systems, reducing his involvement in daily operations. His time commitment drops significantly, allowing him to focus on strategic decisions and personal priorities. With strong cash flow and reduced debt, Daniel reaches financial freedom. His portfolio provides consistent income, and his systems ensure stability.

Daniel now has multiple options. He can continue to hold his properties for long-term income, refinance to access capital, or sell his portfolio for a significant payout. His equity exceeds $2 million, and his business operates efficiently.

This example demonstrates the final stage of multi-unit Airbnb investing. By focusing on optimization, efficiency, and strategic decisions, Daniel achieves mastery and financial freedom.

The key takeaway is that success is not just about growth—it is about reaching a point where your system works for you. By following this path, you can create a portfolio that provides not only income, but freedom, stability, and long-term wealth.

Final Thoughts

As you reach the end of this journey through multi-unit Airbnb mortgage investing, it is important to pause and reflect on what has truly been built here. This is not just a collection of strategies, formulas, or financing techniques. What you now possess is a complete system—a way of thinking, analyzing, structuring, and executing that can be applied again and again to create real, lasting wealth. The true value of this knowledge is not in any single deal, but in your ability to repeat the process with clarity and confidence.

At the beginning of this series, the focus was on understanding the fundamentals—how Airbnb loans work, how income is calculated, and how to qualify. As you progressed, the complexity increased. You learned how to structure deals, analyze multi-unit properties, optimize income, manage risk, scale your portfolio, and ultimately build a system that operates at a high level. Each step built upon the last, creating a foundation that is both strong and flexible.

What makes multi-unit Airbnb investing so powerful is its ability to combine multiple advantages into one strategy. You have the scalability of multi-unit properties, the income potential of short-term rentals, and the leverage of modern financing. When these elements are aligned correctly, they create opportunities that are difficult to replicate in other areas of real estate. This is why so many investors are drawn to this space—and why those who master it are able to achieve extraordinary results.

However, with opportunity comes responsibility. The strategies you have learned require discipline, attention to detail, and a commitment to continuous improvement. Success in this space is not automatic. It is earned through consistent action, thoughtful decision-making, and a willingness to adapt. The market will change, regulations will evolve, and competition will increase. Your ability to stay focused and flexible will determine your long-term success.

One of the most important lessons from this journey is that numbers tell the truth. Every decision you make should be grounded in data and analysis. Whether you are evaluating a new deal, optimizing an existing property, or planning your next move, your numbers provide clarity. They remove emotion from the equation and allow you to make decisions based on reality rather than assumptions. This analytical approach is one of your greatest advantages.

Another key takeaway is the importance of systems. Without systems, growth becomes difficult and inconsistent. With systems, growth becomes scalable and predictable. From guest communication to cleaning, pricing, and financial tracking, every aspect of your business should be structured and repeatable. This not only improves performance but also frees you to focus on higher-level strategy.

Mindset is equally important. The transition from beginner to advanced investor is not just about knowledge—it is about how you think. You begin to see opportunities where others see obstacles. You approach challenges as problems to be solved rather than barriers to progress. This mindset allows you to move forward with confidence, even in uncertain situations.

Risk management has also been a recurring theme throughout this series. The goal is not to avoid risk entirely, but to understand it and manage it effectively. By maintaining reserves, diversifying your portfolio, and planning for different scenarios, you create a foundation that can withstand challenges. This stability allows you to continue growing without being derailed by temporary setbacks.

Scaling is where the real transformation occurs. Moving from one property to multiple properties changes everything. Your income increases, your opportunities expand, and your perspective shifts. You begin to think in terms of systems and portfolios rather than individual deals. This is where the compounding effect of your efforts becomes visible. At the highest level, this journey is about more than money. It is about freedom—freedom to choose how you spend your time, where you live, and what you pursue. It is about creating a life that is not limited by financial constraints. Multi-unit Airbnb investing is simply the vehicle that makes this possible.

Legacy is another important dimension. The system you build can extend beyond your own lifetime, providing opportunities and security for future generations. This requires intentional planning, clear structures, and a commitment to sustainability. When done correctly, your portfolio becomes more than an investment—it becomes a lasting asset.

As you move forward, it is important to remember that progress comes from action. Reading, learning, and planning are essential, but they must be followed by execution. Each deal you analyze, each property you acquire, and each system you implement brings you closer to your goals. The path may not always be linear, but consistent effort will produce results.

You will also encounter challenges. Deals will fall through, markets will shift, and unexpected issues will arise. These experiences are part of the process. Each challenge provides an opportunity to learn and improve. The most successful investors are those who remain persistent and adaptable. Another important concept is patience. Building a portfolio takes time. While it is possible to achieve rapid growth, sustainable success is built over years of consistent effort. Patience allows you to make better decisions, avoid unnecessary risks, and build a stronger foundation.

As you continue this journey, surround yourself with the right people. Lenders, brokers, contractors, and other investors can provide valuable insights and opportunities. Collaboration accelerates growth and helps you navigate challenges more effectively.

Stay committed to learning. The market will continue to evolve, and new tools, strategies, and opportunities will emerge. By staying informed and open to new ideas, you ensure that your approach remains relevant and effective.

Finally, remember why you started. Whether your goal is financial independence, flexibility, or building a legacy, keeping that vision in mind will guide your decisions and keep you motivated. Your portfolio is not just a collection of properties—it is a reflection of your goals and your commitment to achieving them.

This is not the end of the journey—it is the beginning of a new phase. You now have the knowledge and tools to move forward with confidence. The next step is yours to take. The opportunity is real. The system works. The only question that remains is how far you are willing to go.

How to Get a Personalized Airbnb Mortgage Loan Review

If you found this book helpful, you may want to see how these strategies apply to your own financial situation and investment goals. Every investor's profile is unique. Property type, location, projected Airbnb income, credit score, available capital, and lending guidelines all impact what loan programs you may qualify for and how your deal can be structured.

The examples in this book are designed to teach how Airbnb mortgage loans work—but your real options can only be determined by reviewing your specific numbers and investment scenario.

You can request a no-obligation Airbnb mortgage loan consultation here:

Email: info@FinibiMortgage.com

A licensed mortgage professional will review your scenario and explain what Airbnb financing options may be available to you, including DSCR loans, Non-QM programs, and alternative qualification strategies based on your property and financial profile.

No cost. No pressure. No obligation.

Sincerely,

Joseph G. Correa

Licensed Mortgage Loan Originator

Finibi Mortgage Inc.

About the Author

Joseph G. Correa is a licensed mortgage broker and the founder of Finibi Mortgage, a Florida-based brokerage specializing in real estate investment financing, Airbnb and short-term rental loans, and alternative lending strategies for investors, entrepreneurs, and self-employed borrowers. With more than two decades of experience in mortgage lending, underwriting, and financial structuring, Joseph has helped thousands of clients secure funding using intelligent, flexible loan strategies designed for modern real estate investing.

Unlike traditional loan officers who focus only on closing transactions, Joseph's approach is rooted in long-term wealth building. He believes that mortgage financing—especially for Airbnb and investment properties—should be used as a strategic tool to generate cash flow, scale portfolios, and create financial independence. His philosophy centers on using leverage intelligently, allowing investors to grow without relying solely on personal income or traditional lending limitations.

Joseph is widely recognized for his expertise in DSCR loans, Non-QM lending, short-term rental financing, bank statement programs, and creative deal structuring. He specializes in helping investors qualify based on property income rather than personal income, making it possible for beginners, self-employed individuals, and experienced investors to acquire and scale Airbnb portfolios. His ability to simplify complex lending concepts into clear, actionable strategies has empowered countless individuals to enter the real estate market with confidence.

Joseph created *The Airbnb Mortgage Loan Mastery Series* to give investors the same financing knowledge used by banks, private lenders, and institutional real estate operators. His mission is simple: to help people understand how to qualify, structure deals, and scale using modern lending strategies—so they can build profitable Airbnb businesses and long-term wealth.

When he is not structuring deals or writing, Joseph works directly with investors and borrowers across the United States to design customized financing strategies that align with their goals, property types, and growth plans.

The Airbnb Mortgage Loan Mastery Series Roadmap

The Professional Guide to Financing, Scaling, and Profiting from Short-Term Rental Properties

The purpose of *The Airbnb Mortgage Loan Mastery Series* is to give investors the same financing strategies used by banks, lenders, and institutional real estate operators—translated into clear, practical guidance for everyday investors. Each book builds on the last, taking you from foundational knowledge to advanced deal structuring, portfolio scaling, and long-term wealth creation using Airbnb and short-term rental properties.

Book 1 — Airbnb Mortgage Loan Fundamentals This book gives you the foundation. You will understand how Airbnb mortgage loans work, what makes them different from traditional financing, and how lenders evaluate short-term rental properties. You will learn the core concepts of DSCR, Non-QM loans, and income-based qualification, along with who qualifies and how to structure your first deal. Every book that follows builds on this knowledge and shows you how to apply it to real-world investing.

Book 2 — DSCR Airbnb Mortgage Loans This book focuses on one of the most powerful tools in Airbnb investing: DSCR loans. You will learn how to qualify using rental income instead of personal income, how DSCR is calculated using short-term rental data, and how to position your property to meet lender requirements. This book shows you how to break free from traditional income limitations and scale faster.

Book 3 — Airbnb Mortgage Loans for Beginners This book is designed for first-time investors. You will learn how to buy your first Airbnb property using the right loan strategy, how to analyze deals, and how to overcome common obstacles. It provides a clear, step-by-step path from zero experience to your first successful investment.

Book 4 — Airbnb Investment Property Mortgage Loans This book focuses on scaling. You will learn how to finance multiple Airbnb properties, build a portfolio, and optimize cash flow. It introduces strategies for acquiring properties efficiently and managing them as part of a larger system.

Book 5 — Airbnb Mortgage Loans with No Income Verification

This book explores advanced qualification strategies. You will learn how to get approved without tax returns using DSCR, bank statement, and alternative documentation programs. It is designed for self-employed borrowers and investors who want flexibility in how they qualify.

Book 6 — Luxury Airbnb Mortgage Loans

This book focuses on high-end properties. You will learn how to finance luxury Airbnb investments, analyze high average daily rates, and balance risk with return. It introduces jumbo loan strategies and premium market positioning.

Book 7 — Airbnb Mortgage Loans for Vacation Homes

This book explains how to finance second homes and convert them into profitable short-term rentals. You will learn the difference between second home and investment property guidelines, along with hybrid usage strategies and compliance considerations.

Book 8 — Airbnb Mortgage Loan Refinancing & Cash-Out Strategies

This book teaches you how to unlock equity and scale faster. You will learn how to refinance Airbnb properties, execute cash-out strategies, and recycle capital into new investments.

Book 9 — Airbnb Mortgage Loans for Multi-Unit Properties

This book focuses on duplexes, triplexes, and small multifamily properties. You will learn how to finance multiple income streams within one property, analyze mixed rental models, and navigate zoning and compliance.

Book 10 — Advanced Airbnb Mortgage Loan Structuring

This book brings everything together. You will learn how to combine DSCR, asset-based, and creative financing strategies to close complex deals. It is designed for investors who want to operate at a high level and scale without limits.

This series is designed to be followed step by step or used as a reference based on your current stage. Whether you are just starting or already building a portfolio, each book provides the tools, strategies, and insights needed to move forward with clarity and confidence.

The goal is simple: to help you understand how to finance, structure, and scale Airbnb investments so you can build a profitable, long-term real estate business.

Educational & Financial Disclaimer

This book is provided for educational and informational purposes only. The author and publisher are not engaged in rendering legal, tax, accounting, investment, or financial advice. Although Joseph G. Correa is a licensed mortgage loan originator, the information in this book is intended to provide general education about Airbnb mortgage loans, DSCR financing, and short-term rental investment strategies—not personalized financial, legal, or lending advice.

Mortgage programs, underwriting guidelines, interest rates, credit requirements, and short-term rental financing options vary by lender, investor, state, and economic conditions, and may change at any time without notice. The examples, calculations, and scenarios presented in this book are hypothetical and are for illustration purposes only. They do not represent guaranteed results, loan approvals, or actual investment outcomes.

Short-term rental performance, including Airbnb income, occupancy rates, and average daily rates, is influenced by market demand, competition, seasonality, management quality, and local regulations. These factors can vary significantly and are not guaranteed. Before making any financial decisions—including purchasing an Airbnb property, applying for a DSCR or Non-QM loan, refinancing, or using real estate financing for investment purposes—readers should consult with a qualified mortgage professional, financial advisor, tax advisor, or attorney who can evaluate their specific situation.

Risk Disclosure

Real estate investing and short-term rental financing involve risk. Airbnb properties rely on variable income, which can fluctuate due to changes in demand, competition, economic conditions, and local regulations. There is no guarantee that a property will achieve projected income levels or maintain consistent occupancy.

Borrowing to purchase or refinance investment properties increases financial leverage and risk. Failure to make required mortgage payments could result in foreclosure or loss of property. DSCR and Non-QM loans may carry higher interest rates, stricter terms, or prepayment penalties, which can impact long-term profitability.

Additionally, changes in laws or regulations governing short-term rentals may affect your ability to operate a property as an Airbnb. Investors are responsible for ensuring compliance with all local, state, and federal regulations.

This book teaches structured, strategic, and responsible approaches to Airbnb financing and investing, but no strategy is risk-free. Readers are solely responsible for their financial decisions and outcomes. Neither the author nor the publisher makes any warranties, express or implied, regarding the accuracy, completeness, or applicability of the information in this book to any individual situation.

www.ingramcontent.com/pod-product-compliance
Lightning Source LLC
LaVergne TN
LVHW022224200926
848481LV00006B/2106